LEADERSHIP STYLES

How to Discover and Leverage Yours

Mark Murphy

Founder of Leadership IQ

To Andrea, Isabella, and Andrew

FOR MORE INFORMATION

For free downloadable resources including quizzes and discussion guides, please visit www.leadershipiq.com

TABLE OF CONTENTS

INTRODUCTION

A recent survey of presidential historians ranked Franklin Delano Roosevelt and Dwight D. Eisenhower as America's third and fifth best presidents, respectively. Outside of any personal political persuasion, experts generally agree that Roosevelt and Eisenhower were both immensely skilled leaders. That these two men were highly effective leaders is of great interest, but it's the stylistic differences in leadership each used to achieve that effectiveness that really stands out.

With his inspirational style and political guile, Roosevelt rallied the nation to success through unprecedented economic and military struggles. A communicator par excellence, he sensed what people needed to hear and when they needed to hear it. Over his twelve years in office, and as he led the nation through the crises of the Great Depression and World War II, Roosevelt's "Fireside Chats" connected the White House to everyday Americans as never before. With political and communicative deftness, he addressed and assuaged America's fears and aspirations. He challenged people to surmount existential threats, sacrifice for the greater good, and in doing so, restored the nation's faith in their government.

Yet, as Princeton historian Fred Greenstein notes, Roosevelt's predilection for political maneuvering carried over into his relations with his staff. One of his aides remarked:

He seemed not to want any one person to know the whole story. At times he seemed to delight in having two or more people do different but related parts of a single job that could have been done by one person...it frequently led to duplication of effort and sometimes to argument and conflict.[1]

Roosevelt was a political genius, a savant at diagnosing power dynamics and, perhaps because of these gifts, a master manipulator. But his machinations continued to roil a notoriously chaotic organization that sometimes undercut his own policy initiatives. Between pitting aides against one another and challenging them with seemingly impossible tasks, he hurt morale, wasted countless hours of his staff's time, and even reduced the quality of the policy expertise he was provided.

Ultimately, much like a jazz virtuoso with a bit of a drinking problem, Roosevelt's genius exceeded his failings. Absent structural deficiencies and excessive manipulation of staff, the 32nd president's accomplishments might have been even greater.

On the opposite end of the leadership style spectrum, we find Eisenhower. Where the former was unstructured, improvisational, inscrutable, yet wildly inspirational, Eisenhower entered the White House with more operational expertise and gravitas than any president before or since. As the former supreme allied commander in Europe in World War II, Eisenhower knew structure better than anyone.

He created rules and policies that fostered stability and predictability. Far from Roosevelt's chaos, Eisenhower chose his people carefully, monitored and evaluated their performance, and made adjustments as warranted. But he wasn't a mere plodder, hidebound to antiquated policy; he was an innovator. In *The Presidential Difference,* Fred Greenstein's instructive account of the presidential qualities that have served well and poorly in the Oval

Office, he informs readers that Eisenhower created the first White House chief of staff, the first congressional relations office, and the first presidential assistant for national security affairs (what we today call the national security advisor).

Eisenhower enlisted three groups of experienced national security analysts in a year-long deliberation to rethink our national strategy to achieve "security without paying the price of national bankruptcy." With each group providing drastically different strategies, he availed himself of the best possible thinking, and arguably, he precisely honed and modernized the discipline of scenario planning. Interestingly, not only did this process develop greater insight, it also stimulated team building and collaboration.

Eisenhower's genius for structure, organization, and staff cohesion are to be as admired as Roosevelt's talent for inspiring, challenging and understanding people. And as Roosevelt's impressive strengths occasionally became weaknesses, so too did Eisenhower's talents for structure cause intermittent trouble.

When the Soviet Union successfully launched Sputnik in 1957, Americans went into a panic over a perceived technological gap between the United States and Soviet Union. Eisenhower's response was to send out his press secretary to undermine the Soviet's accomplishment—followed by his Secretary of Defense—and then, his Chief of Staff. Eisenhower himself didn't respond until five days later. Because of his military acumen, he knew that Sputnik was a much smaller threat than the average citizen imagined, but his deliberative nature and steady calm failed to convince the American people that they had nothing to fear. A touch of Roosevelt's political savvy might have been very helpful here.

Lest there be any doubt; I am a huge admirer of both presidents. They were extraordinary leaders, and while both had strengths and weaknesses, they achieved remarkable successes. And of greatest interest for us is that they both achieved success with wildly different leadership styles.

Roosevelt's intense challenging of his staff and Eisenhower's structure and stability are all elements of a leader's style. Some leaders challenge their reports to expend maximal energy, while others are fine with sub-herculean efforts. Some leaders favor stability and predictability; others like the adrenaline rush that comes with rapid change. Some like to retain final authority for making critical decisions, while others are more comfortable spreading that authority. And some are deeply concerned about the personal needs of their employees, while others prefer to maintain emotional distance.

THE FOUR COMPONENTS OF LEADERSHIP STYLE

After years of study, involving more than 300,000 leaders, my research team and I have discovered that there are four components of leadership style: Feeling, Challenge, Structure and Directiveness.

A leader high in Feeling regularly asks employees about their motivators and demotivators, cares deeply about the personal needs of employees, supports an environment in which employees genuinely like one another, and is concerned that employees find their work personally fulfilling.

A leader high in Challenge pushes employees to develop their weaknesses and not just focus on their strengths, and pushes employees to give maximal, 100% effort.

A leader high in Directiveness retains the final decision-making authority, tells employees exactly how they would like tasks and projects to be performed, works harder and longer than anyone else on the team, and clearly communicates to employees the consequences of unsatisfactory work.

And a leader high in Structure emphasizes formal procedures, rules, and policies, and emphasizes stability and predictability.

If these descriptions appear a bit technical, it's because they are. Phrases such as, "pushes employees to give maximal effort," "emphasizes stability and predictability," and "cares deeply about the personal needs of employees," are drawn from surveys and assessments that we've used to evaluate leaders, including how followers view leaders' behavior, how leaders see themselves, and even people's idealized versions of leaders. These phrases aren't mere collections of words; they're specific and tested descriptors of different aspects of a leader's behavior and beliefs.

As you'll learn in this book, these four components are mixed and matched in a variety of configurations to form four distinct leadership styles. For example, with his intensely challenging tasks and lower regard for his staff's feelings, Roosevelt falls into the Pragmatist leadership style. By contrast, Eisenhower's clear delineation of how he wanted things done, alongside his formal procedures, rules, and policies, place him into the Steward leadership style. Diplomat and Idealist are the other two leadership styles.

But before we start to explore these leadership styles, it is critically important to point out that these four components (Feeling, Challenge, Structure and Directiveness) are neither wholly bad nor good. Being "structured" can provide reassurance in one setting but feel stifling in another. There are times when "challenging" someone to deliver 100% effort is the only way to accomplish a goal, and other occasions when such high levels of exertion cause burnout and demoralization. Even a characteristic that seems universally positive, like "feeling," is ill-suited to particular leadership environments, e.g., an organization in such dire financial straits that the only way to salvage the firm is to dispassionately dismiss half of the workforce.

We will return, shortly, to exploring how these components form distinct leadership styles, but I will first address a critical topic, known as "leadership universals."

LEADERSHIP UNIVERSALS

Most people want a leader who evidences a modicum of common decency, tolerates at least a bit of disagreement, and minimally shares some occasional good news. These are fundamental leadership behaviors that most followers desire and that, ideally, are embraced by all leaders, regardless of their leadership style.

There are also leadership behaviors that are fundamentally bad. I regularly receive emails from managers whose bosses are mentally and cognitively unfit to be leaders, and they'll ask something like, "Is there a leadership style that encompasses 'crazy?'" The answer is simply, "No." To even enter the discussion about one's leadership style, a person must first demonstrate some foundational mental, emotional and cognitive competence. We can discuss Roosevelt and Eisenhower's leadership style because, even though they both made mistakes, they were mentally, emotionally and cognitively competent.

Perhaps you've witnessed someone in a leadership role who didn't cope well with ordinary stresses such as basic criticism or unflattering news. Or they lacked a basic grip on reality. Or they consistently demonstrated belligerent, instigating and vitriolic behavior. A person like that does not have a leadership style; they don't even deserve the moniker of leader. They may hold an impressive title, but they are not a leader. And aside from the rare masochist, no one loves following someone who displays those kinds of behaviors.

In addition to issues of basic competence, my research has identified ten "leadership universals." While these ten behaviors are critical for everyone in a leadership role to know and practice, I don't include these "leadership universals" in discussions of leadership style because there is hardly anyone who doesn't require these from their leader.

Here are the 10 leadership universals...

1. The leader generally gives employees constructive feedback, face-to-face or over the phone, rather than via email or text.

2. When communicating a decision, the leader generally shares how they came to this conclusion.
3. The leader shares good and bad news.
4. When an employee makes an error, the leader immediately provides constructive feedback, rather than waiting days or weeks.
5. The leader encourages employees to share their opinions, even if they have radically different points of view.
6. When something goes wrong, the leader asks for advice from employees on how to fix it.
7. The leader openly shares the mistakes they've made.
8. The leader typically doesn't avoid conflict or uncomfortable conversations.
9. The leader tolerates at least some disagreement or questioning.
10. The leader considers suggestions made by employees.

Most of these behaviors seem obvious. Across hundreds of thousands of survey respondents, 99% say they would like their leader to speak with them directly, or via telephone, when they deliver constructive feedback. This mode of communication fosters a two-way conversation, misinterpretations are less likely to occur or are more easily corrected and, frankly, criticizing someone via email can appear cowardly.

Similarly, 99% would like to understand the process by which their leader came to make important decisions. We might not always agree with a leader's decisions, but people are generally more agreeable and willing to follow if they understand how those decisions were made. All leaders, even the most lauded ones, make bad decisions. Equally, all leaders sometimes make great decisions that, for reasons unknown or unanticipated, deliver terrible results. But those decisional mistakes are generally forgiven when followers understand the logic and rationale behind them.

Not everyone desires a leader who fosters an environment in which people genuinely like one another; some people like to compete with their colleagues. Not everyone desires a leader who pushes people to fix their weaknesses; some people would rather just use their existing strengths. Not everyone desires a leader who retains the final decision-making authority; some people prefer a more democratic environment. However, virtually everyone desires to:

- Hear constructive feedback face-to-face, within hours, not weeks.
- Understand their leader's decision-making processes, including those that resulted in mistakes.
- Hear both good and bad news; and to have their opinions solicited and heard, even when those opinions represent a challenge to the leader

Leaders have broad stylistic freedom in how they incorporate those universal behaviors, but incorporate them they must.

THE FOUR LEADERSHIP STYLES

Here's what we know so far. First, before a leader can be thought of as having a style, that leader must be mentally, emotionally and cognitively competent. Second, there are universal behaviors that every leader should perform, regardless of their stylistic predilections. And third, assuming that we've satisfied the first two criteria, there are the four aforementioned components of a leader's style: Feeling, Challenge, Structure and Directiveness.

Feeling, Challenge, Structure and Directiveness can be mixed and matched in a variety of ways. For example, Roosevelt was high in Challenge and lower in Feeling, while Eisenhower was high in Structure and Directiveness and lower in Challenge. Leaders can demonstrate strong or weak tendencies in one or more of these areas. But, after the study of more than 300,000 leaders, employing a variety of statistical techniques, including factor analysis and k-means clustering, we have discovered that there are four distinct clusters of these characteristics, and that those clusters form the leadership styles.

For example, it's theoretically possible for a leader to be high in Structure and Feeling and low in Directiveness and Challenge, but out in the real world, it's not a combination of characteristics we often find. It's tough to even imagine how those combined characteristics would manifest in real life. They would have a multitude of formal procedures and rules but not communicate to employees exactly how they would like tasks to be performed—a very odd mixture.

Here's a brief look at the four leadership styles that we most commonly see in the field. [Note: For a deeper look at our research methodology, visit www.leadershipiq.com/leadership-styles]

The Pragmatist

Pragmatists rate very high on Challenge, moderately high on Directiveness and Structure, and much lower on Feeling. The Pragmatist pushes employees to address and correct weaknesses, not focus only on their strengths, and to deliver maximal, 100% effort. But it's not just their employees; these leaders typically work harder and longer than anyone else on the team. Being a Pragmatist also commonly involves telling employees exactly how tasks and projects are to be performed and clearly communicating the consequences of unsatisfactory work. They may also push the envelope in terms of formal procedures, rules, and policies to get what they want.

Pragmatists have high standards, and they expect themselves, and their employees, to meet those standards. They are driven and competitive, and value hitting their goals above all else. They can be bold thinkers, unafraid of taking the road less traveled, even when others struggle or feel anxious. They are also determined, single-minded, and often enjoy smashing through obstacles. The Pragmatist's number one priority is getting the job, project or task done.

The Diplomat
Diplomats rate high in Feeling and much lower in Challenge, Structure and Directiveness. The Diplomat regularly asks employees about their motivators and demotivators, cares deeply about the personal needs of employees, supports an environment in which employees genuinely like one another, and is very concerned that employees find their work personally fulfilling.

Diplomats prize interpersonal harmony. They are the social glue and affiliative force that keeps groups together. Diplomats are kind, social, and giving, and typically build deep personal bonds with their employees. They are often known for being able to resolve conflicts peacefully, and for avoiding conflicts in the first place. The Diplomat's number one priority is ensuring that their followers enjoy their jobs.

The Steward
Stewards rate high in Structure and Directiveness and low in Challenge and Feeling. The Steward emphasizes formal procedures, rules, and policies, and emphasizes stability and predictability. The Steward typically retains the final decision-making authority, tells employees exactly how they would like tasks and projects to be performed, works harder and longer than anyone else on the team, and clearly communicates to employees the consequences of unsatisfactory work.

Stewards are the rocks of organizations. They're dependable, loyal and helpful, and they provide a stabilizing and calming force for their employees. Stewards value rules, process and cooperation. They believe that a chain is only as strong as its weakest link, and they move only as fast as the entire chain will allow, taking care and time to help those who struggle to keep up. The Steward's number one priority is ensuring that the operation runs efficiently and effectively.

The Idealist

Idealists rate high in Feeling and Challenge, and lower in Structure and Directiveness. Like the Pragmatist, the Idealist pushes employees to develop their weaknesses, and not just focus on their strengths, and pushes employees to give maximal, 100% effort. But the Idealist balances that challenging with high levels of Feeling. The Idealist regularly asks employees about their motivators and demotivators, cares deeply about the personal needs of employees, wants an environment in which employees genuinely like one another, and is very concerned that employees find their work personally fulfilling. In many ways, the Idealist is like the high-school teacher who tells students, "I'm gonna push you hard, but I'm doing this because I care about you and want to see you succeed."

Idealists are high-energy achievers who believe in the positive potential of everyone around them. Idealists want to learn and grow, and they want everyone else on the team to do the same. They are often charismatic, drawing others to them with their intuition and idealism. They're open-minded and prize creativity from themselves and others. The Idealist's number one priority is seeing that their followers grow and develop.

THE BIG A-HA!

Contrary to what most leadership books would have you believe, there is not one right way or one perfect approach to be a successful leader. Yes, there are the leadership universals, but there is a lot more to good leadership than only those ten behaviors. Roosevelt and Eisenhower were both incredibly successful leaders, but their styles were a study in contrasts. As we'll see throughout the book, leaders like Tim Cook from Apple, Sheryl Sandberg from Facebook, and Jeff Bezos from Amazon, are all successful leaders with wildly different approaches.

It seems intuitively obvious that leaders should embody and employ different styles; companies aren't all the same, so why should their leaders be the same? And yet, every year there are a wealth of leadership books purporting to illuminate the "one path" to great leadership. It's an absurd conceit, and a damaging one. The leadership style that works best for a team of ambitious, competitive go-getters (the Pragmatist) is not the style that works best for a group of affiliative collaborators (the Diplomat) or detail-oriented, rule-followers (the Steward).

Truly great leaders understand their leadership style, when to embrace it fully or dial it back, in which environments they are most likely to succeed, and how to choose followers who fit well with their leadership style. These are precisely the subjects that I address in this book.

WHAT COMES NEXT

Thus far I've provided only brief descriptions of the four leadership styles. The following four chapters will take a deep look at each of the leadership styles. We'll explore each style's strengths and weaknesses, situations in which the leadership style works well, signs that the style is not working, what types of employees work well with each style, and practical techniques for utilizing that leadership style.

Before you begin, I would encourage you to assess your own leadership style by visiting our website at www.leadershipiq.com/leadership-styles.

CHAPTER 1
THE PRAGMATIST

In mid-2016, Tesla co-founder and CEO Elon Musk sent an email to all employees that read, in part, as follows:

> I thought it was important to write you a note directly to let you know how critical this quarter is. **The third quarter will be our last chance to show investors** that Tesla can be at least slightly positive cash flow and profitable before the Model 3 reaches full production. Once we get to Q4, Model 3 capital expenditures force us into a negative position until Model 3 reaches full production. That won't be until late next year.
>
> We are on the razor's edge of achieving a good Q3, but **it requires building and delivering every car we possibly can, while simultaneously trimming any cost that isn't critical**, at least for the next 4.5 weeks. Right now, we are tracking to be a few percentage points negative on cash flow and GAAP profitability, but this is a small number, so I'm confident that **we can rally hard** and push the results into positive territory. **It would be awesome to throw a pie**

in the face of all the naysayers on Wall Street who keep insisting that Tesla will always be a money-loser![1]

The boldface is mine, for emphasis, and I use it because when you hear a leader use phrases like "last chance," "build while simultaneously trimming," "rally hard," or "throw a pie in the face of…" to motivate the troops, it's a good sign that you're hearing the Pragmatist leadership style at work.

THE PRAGMATIST STYLE DEFINED

Pragmatists rate very high on Challenge, moderately high on Directiveness and Structure, and much lower on Feeling. Overall, when we chart Pragmatists' scores on these four factors, they look something like the following (the bars represent the range of scores for each of the factors with the lines inside the bars representing where the majority of scores fall):

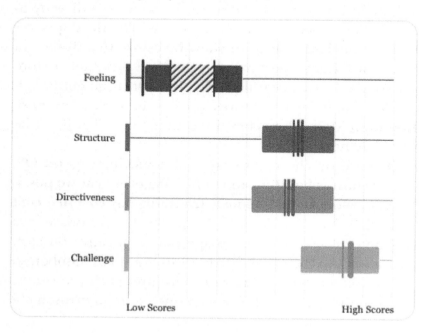

Rating high on Challenge means that the Pragmatist pushes employees to work on strengthening their weaknesses, not just focus only on their strengths, and to give maximal, 100% effort. The Pragmatist doesn't ask employees to do anything that they're not willing to do themselves. They typically work harder and longer than anyone else on the team. Elon Musk, a famously hard-working CEO, certainly challenges his people to a high level of performance in his 2016 email, but he has also admitted in interviews to personally putting in long hours, even up to 100-hour work weeks, to achieve his big goals.

The Pragmatist is not someone who gives assignments and, as long as the work gets done well, leaves it up to the employee to determine how. Pragmatists are directive and structured, and people who work for a Pragmatist can expect to receive clear and detailed instructions on exactly how tasks and projects should be performed. This typically includes equally strong communications regarding performance expectations and the consequences of unsatisfactory work. Pragmatists know what they want and how they want it done, and they won't hesitate to push the envelope on formal procedures, rules, and policies to get it.

Rating low on Feeling means that the Pragmatist won't often ask about employee motivators and demotivators. There isn't much focus on the personal needs of employees or importance placed on building an environment in which employees genuinely like one another. This doesn't make Pragmatists nasty people; they're just more heavily focused on meeting their goals than they are on meeting the immediate emotional wants of their employees.

It's important to note that I refer to "immediate" emotional wants, because there's a legitimate school of thought, to which Pragmatists often subscribe, that posits true happiness comes only after significant achievements. Sure, you can live a life of balance and gratitude and mindfulness, but this will never earn you the profound, life-altering gratification of, say, climbing Mount

Everest, or putting yourself through an arduous graduate program, or founding an electric car company. For many Pragmatists, only HARD Goals[2], goals with the right element of difficulty that push us to achieve the "impossible," can deliver that level of true deep fulfillment.

Pragmatists want fulfillment and happiness as much as most human beings do, but they tend to be willing to pay the price of short-term suffering far more than do those who utilize some of the other leadership styles. Jeff Bezos, founder and CEO of Amazon, and in my assessment a Pragmatist, addresses this in the following excerpt from an interview he gave on risk-taking and customer value. Once again, the boldface type is mine and it's used to show emphasis:

> ...we are going to be bold with our experiments and some of them aren't going to work. If you know they're going to work they're not experiments. And if you decide that you are only going to do things that you know are going to work, you're going to leave a lot of opportunity on the table. Companies are rarely criticized for the things that they failed to try.
>
> And they are, many times, criticized for things they tried and failed at. And that's one of the reasons, **if you want to be a pioneer, you have to get comfortable being misunderstood. In some ways it's a much more pleasant life, probably, we wouldn't know from personal experience, to not - you know, once you have something good just to hone it and hone it and hone it and not try anything new.**[3]

In the interview, Jeff says that it's probably "a much more pleasant life" to not try anything new. However, when you look at Amazon's track record of ongoing innovation, it's easy to suppose that he does believe that trying new things is worth any short-term discomfort or suffering. Jeff himself says that he encourages employees "to go down blind alleys and experiment,"[4] and in true Pragmatist style, he doesn't sugarcoat the reality that challenging yourself and others to pursue incredibly HARD Goals is not always going to be fun, especially in the short term.

Pragmatists are often bold thinkers, unafraid of taking the road less traveled, even when others struggle, feel anxious or think that the Pragmatist's goals are "idiocy squared." Elon Musk is considered by many people as one of Silicon Valley's most adventurous entrepreneurs and he exemplifies this kind of bold thinking. From building a superhighway to the Moon to colonizing Mars, Elon doesn't set his sights on average goals. Tell him that something is a safe bet, and it's a safe bet that he won't want to do it.

Blogging about Tesla's founding, Elon wrote:

> I thought our chances of success were so low that I didn't want to risk anyone's funds in the beginning but my own. The list of successful car company startups is short. As of 2016, the number of American car companies that haven't gone bankrupt is a grand total of two: Ford and Tesla. Starting a car company is idiotic and an electric car company is idiocy squared.[5]

It's not everyone who will invest their own millions into an endeavor that has a strong track record of failure. But when you consider that Elon's definition of success, shared by many Pragmatists, includes changing the world, then you begin to understand the drive behind taking such a high level of risk.

It is hard-driving Pragmatists whom we so often see smashing through truly tough obstacles, and it's not because they don't get nervous or are immune to fear. Speaking at the Dublin Web Summit in 2013, Elon remarked about the fourth launch of

SpaceX (following three failures to launch), "I was so tense that when it succeeded I didn't actually feel elation—just stress relief, that's all."[6]

Pragmatists feel fear and worry about failure just like everyone else, but their drive, competitiveness, high standards, and the fact that they value hitting their goals above all else, help to move them past those fears. As you might expect, when working for a Pragmatist, you're expected to embrace many of these same qualities.

Working for Pragmatists can be difficult but rewarding. The job is intense and not for the faint-of-heart or the thin-skinned. Bottom-line results will always outpace softer measures such as employee engagement, but the opportunities to learn and become expert under the Pragmatist's tutelage are second to none. The job can sometimes feel like an apprenticeship to a master artist or professor. Elite performers who like to be pushed hard and who are looking for the potential for exceptional intellectual growth do best working for the Pragmatist, but they won't be immune to the real potential for burnout and criticism.

In Elon Musk's 2016 email to employees, he states point blank, "We are on the razor's edge of achieving a good Q3, but it requires building and delivering every car we possibly can, while simultaneously trimming any cost that isn't critical." You'll note that he doesn't ask his employees to share their personal needs, nor does he say how important it is that everyone who works at Tesla genuinely like one another. His message is clear, and it essentially says, "We've got two really hard tasks (deliver cars and cut costs)—and they're made even harder because we're doing them simultaneously…but hey, that's what we're here to do!"

You may have noticed that the language used in Elon and Jeff's quotes is very direct. It's not uncommon for Pragmatists to be quite blunt in conversation, while leaders who are not Pragmatists often employ more temperate language. While a Pragmatist might say, "It would be awesome to throw a pie in the face of all the naysayers on Wall Street…," a Diplomat might phrase it a bit more subtly, perhaps by saying "It's a great opportunity to change the minds of those who have doubted our capabilities."

There are exceptions to the Pragmatists' bluntness. FDR, for example, had the leadership characteristics of a Pragmatist, but when speaking, whether it was telling the nation, "The only thing to fear is fear itself," during his inaugural address, or speaking to the American people informally during his fireside chats, the 32nd president was eloquence exemplified. One rhetorical strategy isn't necessarily better than another, but if you're looking for colorful language and pointed quotes, especially in today's modern business world, Pragmatists are typically the most reliable source.

If you're thinking that not everyone can be an Elon Musk or a Jeff Bezos, then you are correct. My research shows that the Pragmatist style is the least common of all the leadership styles. Interestingly, top-level executives include a higher percentage of Pragmatists than do other groups, such as Managers, Directors and Vice Presidents.

STRENGTHS AND WHERE THE PRAGMATIST STYLE WORKS BEST

All leadership styles work better in some contexts than in others. For example, the hard-charging Pragmatist might not have the ideal style to lead workers who are six months from retirement and who have explicitly said that they want only to transfer their knowledge to younger employees, complete their current projects, and ride off into the sunset. The Pragmatist probably won't get very far pushing these employees to work on their weaknesses or to give maximal effort. However, there are many contexts in which the Pragmatist does shine, including when:

- There are really big goals to achieve.
- Followers are comfortable taking some risks.
- Followers respect the leader.

- There is opportunity to learn.
- The leader works harder than anyone else.
- The leader has titular, formal power.
- Followers are emotionally healthy and not burnt out.
- The leader is not following in the footsteps of a legendary Pragmatist.

Let's take a deeper look at each of those contexts...

There Are Really Big Goals to Achieve

When someone tells me, "I'm a Pragmatist," my first response is usually, "That's great, what's the big goal you're pursuing?" The reason I ask this is because the Pragmatist leadership style is most likely to be successful when there's a HARD Goal to be achieved—something inspiring, meaningful, audacious and difficult.

I'm sure you remember Winston Churchill's famous challenge for the citizens of the United Kingdom: "Whatever the cost may be, we shall fight on the beaches, we shall fight on the landing grounds, we shall fight in the fields and in the streets, we shall fight in the hills; we shall never surrender." Churchill wasn't seeking a small goal, such as a slight increase in governmental efficiency, or asking citizens to reduce energy consumption by 2%, when he uttered these now famous words; he was battling for the survival of Western civilization.

Not every Pragmatist is fighting for humanity's survival, but if you spend any time around most Pragmatists, you'd be forgiven for thinking that they are. In a 1985 Playboy interview, Steve Jobs uttered his famous "dent in the universe" line. While his exact words have been misquoted countless times, what he actually said in reference to the types of people that Apple was hiring is still pretty audacious:

At Apple, people are putting in 18-hour days. We attract a different type of person: a person who doesn't want to wait five or ten years to have someone take a giant risk on him or her. Someone who really wants to get in a little over his head and make a little dent in the universe. We are aware that we are doing something significant. We are here at the beginning of it and were able to shape how it goes. Everyone here has the sense that right now is one of those moments when we are influencing the future.[7]

Imagine instead that Steve had said, "We're working eighteen-hour days because we think that we can reduce the fees you pay at the ATM from three dollars to two dollars." Does that statement rise to the level of making a little "dent in the universe?" Probably not. This is the hurdle that the Pragmatist must clear.

There are people—generally ambitious, driven people—who are more than willing to log long workdays, even eighteen-hour days, when needed, to shore up their weaknesses and to deliver maximal effort. But if they are not convinced that they're doing it in service of something meaningful, worthwhile, audacious and difficult, then they will typically lose interest quickly.

Way back in 1997, Jeff Bezos' Letter to Shareholders included a paragraph that might be considered a de facto mission statement for Pragmatists:

> It's not easy to work here (when I interview people I tell them, "You can work long, hard, or smart, but at Amazon. com you can't choose two out of three"), but we are working to build something important, something that matters to our customers, something that we can all tell our grandchildren about. Such things aren't meant to be easy. We are incredibly fortunate to have this group of dedicated employees whose sacrifices and passion build Amazon.com.[8]

A Pragmatist is at high risk of failure if they're pushing and challenging people to increase the efficiency of Testing Procedure

Specification (TPS) reports by 5%, or a similarly mundane assignment. Imagine that you've been assigned to lead a task force at work and your goal is to create a plan to save the company 4% a year on supply costs. You earnestly tell your colleagues, "We should all plan on working late nights, weekends and holidays for the next six months because this is by far our most important priority!" You're likely to face bemused looks and maybe even a wisecracker or two who asks, "Are you out of your mind? This is a perfunctory task force. We're gonna cut back on free sodas in the breakroom, change overnight shipping to 2-day, and we're done. You can go stick your late nights and weekends!"

People will allow the Pragmatist to push them to their limits, but only if they believe strongly in the goal or vision that hard work represents. If people think the goal is boring, mundane, or not worth significant effort, then the Pragmatist leadership style is liable to be met with eye-rolls or outright resistance.

Followers Are Comfortable Taking Some Risks

It is not out of character for a Pragmatist to challenge employees to, in Steve Jobs' parlance, "make a dent in the universe." Some will see that as fun and exciting—a grand adventure, but others will interpret that universe-denting as risky, dicey or even hazardous to their careers. And as you might imagine, Pragmatists are significantly more successful when their followers are excited by, rather than scared of, big challenges.

Some people love pursuing big challenges even when there is risk involved. For them, the potential upside is more compelling than any downside. Or they just love the adrenaline rush that comes from the gamble. But, for however many there are who love taking risks, there are more who avoid risk, or take only very small risks, and that's an important caution for Pragmatists to heed.

In one of my studies, I asked more than 10,000 people to select from these three options:

- I like taking risks.
- I would take a risk if it seemed prudent.
- I avoid risks.

Only about 28% of respondents said that they like taking risks. If you're a Pragmatist and you're challenging people to pursue an audacious goal that they find risky, then you're prone to run into problems if only 28% of people like taking risks. However, I discovered big differences in how people viewed change when I dissected the data by position. For instance, 40% of top executives like taking risks. But for frontline employees, that number is only 24%. In the average company, the CEO is 66% more apt to enjoy taking risks than the employees.

There are several lessons for Pragmatists here: First, there is a reason that so many famous Pragmatists are CEOs (e.g., Bezos, Jobs or Musk) or world leaders (e.g., FDR and Churchill). People who have risen to these positions are simply more likely to embrace hard, audacious goals and challenge themselves to achieve no matter the cost.

Second, if your hard, audacious goal seems risky, especially in the eyes of employees, then you are probably going to have trouble generating lots of support. You might look at the riskiness and think, "Wow, this is really cool—finally, some excitement!" But given what the above data shows, it's expected that your employees don't view the riskiness quite so favorably and thus might resist your Pragmatist leadership style.

Third, if you're the Pragmatist leader who is challenging your team to achieve this HARD Goal, then you probably have a very different assessment of what constitutes "risk" than do your employees. To you, this challenge might seem like the easiest thing ever, but are the people you lead going to see it that way?

As an example, consider that to an Olympic long-jumper, leaping across a ten-foot wide stream filled with piranhas seems easy.

The world long-jump record is over twenty-nine feet, so it's safe to assume that an Olympic long-jumper can leap ten feet without breaking a sweat. But I probably can't leap ten feet. Asking me to leap across a ten-foot wide stream filled with piranhas is pretty much the same as asking me to jump right into the middle of a stream filled with piranhas. For a world-class athlete, this jump doesn't involve any risk at all; but, for someone like me, it is all risk with virtually no chance of success.

I'm not saying that Pragmatists shouldn't enjoy taking risks. Or that they shouldn't pursue audacious goals, even risky ones. But I am saying that Pragmatists need to be cognizant of the gap between their perception of risk and that of their employees. Because no matter how hard Pragmatists challenge people, if their followers are paralyzed with risk-induced fear, then their leadership approach is likely to fail.

Followers Respect the Leader

The Pragmatist is a challenger who pushes people to improve their weaknesses and requires that they put forth maximal effort. But in order for people to follow a Pragmatist, and deliver that level of performance, they need to believe that those efforts will result in a payoff. If the Pragmatist's competency or judgement is under question, then employees aren't going to trust that their maximal effort will pay off. Belief in a leader stems from respecting that leader.

Imagine you're a Pragmatist and you're joining a new company. You achieved great success in your previous job by pushing and challenging your team. Maybe those team members doubted and resisted you at first, but eventually you persuaded and spurred them to greatness. But now, you're taking over a team that knows nothing of your past accomplishments. Of course, you know how smart you are, and you know that you can awaken the potential in employees of every performance level, but these new followers are oblivious to your leadership skills.

Will you be able to push this new team as hard as you pushed your previous team? Probably not, because they don't yet feel the same level of respect for you. Pragmatists entering new leadership situations must be careful to not push harder than their followers' respect for them will allow. And that's why the next contextual factor is also so important.

There Is Opportunity to Learn
We know that the Pragmatist leadership style works well when there are audacious goals to be achieved. Similarly, this style works well when there are significant learning opportunities for followers.

Think about all of the budding athletes and musicians who willingly subject themselves to incredibly demanding coaches and teachers. Why do these kids embrace this de facto Pragmatist style that holds them to multiple hours of intensive daily practice? Maybe some cases are the result of demanding parents, but typically it's because these kids want to learn and master their particular discipline. Any aspiring pianist, gymnast, dancer, singer, basketball player, etc., knows that to progress from apprentice to master requires maximal effort, and typically, a coach or teacher who requires such effort.

But the example of the budding pianist begs the question, "How similar is the typical employee to an aspiring virtuoso or future Olympian?" Sadly, the answer is typically, "Not very similar." While there should be no shortage of learning opportunities in the modern workplace, according to one of my studies, only 26% of employees say that they're "Always" learning something new at work. Meanwhile, a whopping 39% say they're "Never" or "Rarely" learning new things.[9]

If your environment offers opportunities for followers to significantly expand their minds and skills, the Pragmatist leadership style may nicely approximate the demanding style of so many Olympic coaches; but, sans the potential for significant growth, the Pragmatist style may feel unduly harsh.

The Leader Works Harder than Anyone Else

Pragmatists tend to work as hard, and often harder, than anyone else on their team. The Pragmatist's work ethic and drive stem partly from their psychological makeup. The psychology that causes a person to believe in the value of challenging others generally corresponds to believing in the value of challenging oneself.

But the other source of the Pragmatist's commitment to working long hours is a simply practical consideration; the need to inspire their followers. There's a risk of hypocrisy for all leadership styles. If you're a process-driven leader who admonishes your staff to follow the rules, your exhortations will fall on deaf ears if your team doesn't believe that you follow those same rules. If you're a leader who extols the benefits of a collaborative and collegial work environment, then you risk revolt if you don't commit to the same paradigm. So too, it is with the Pragmatist; if you're pushing your team to give maximal effort, while simultaneously cutting out of the office early, your chances of evoking maximal effort from your team are slim.

In theory, if you're compensating your team fairly to work long hours and put forth lots of effort, then it shouldn't matter whether or not you also work long hours. But in the real world, followers do attend to the signals, especially the non-monetary ones, sent by their leaders. And if those signals even hint at hypocrisy, then followers' motivation drops precipitously.

Legendary investor Mark Cuban was very sincere when he said, "You have to re-earn your customers' business every day, or someone will take that business from you. It's a numbers game.

You have to put in the hours to be prepared, and the hours networking and communicating with prospects and customers. The more effort you put in, the more money you will make." [10]

The Leader Has Titular, Formal Power

There are numerous power sources available to leaders. For example, nearly sixty years ago, psychologists John R. P. French and Bertram Raven identified five sources of power; legitimate, expert, reward, coercion, and referent.

Legitimate, or titular power, comes from having a title or occupying a place in a hierarchy. I have more power as CEO than I did as vice president, more power as vice president than I did as a manager, and so forth. A person with expert power can do things better than others, i.e., has a particular area of expertise. When someone says "I don't know how to work XYZ software. Who's our expert at that? Bob's the expert, Sally's the expert. Let's go ask them because they know how to do it," they are calling upon expert power.

The reason I'm highlighting legitimate and expert sources of power is that they are the ones generally required for the effective utilization of the Pragmatist leadership style. Even artful Pragmatists, at times, push their followers too hard, moving beyond the point where the follower is a willing participant. In those cases, it's very helpful to have legitimate or titular power to wrest that last bit of effort from followers. Jeff Bezos is said to have once remarked, "Do I need to go down and get the certificate that says I'm CEO of the company to get you to stop challenging me on this?" [11] Bezos is about as esteemed as a business leader gets, and yet, even he must occasionally resort to playing the CEO card.

Expert power is the other power source that Pragmatists must cultivate. As noted previously, when people respect the Pragmatist leader, endorse the audacious goals to be achieved and experience personal enrichment, they will follow that leader readily.

Additionally, the more expert the leader, and the more lauded the leader's prodigious skills, the more enthusiastic followers will be in their desire to follow that leader.

Followers Are Emotionally Healthy and Not Burnt Out

According to the Mayo Clinic, burnout is a state of physical, emotional or mental exhaustion combined with doubts about your competence and the value of your work.[12] It takes a mentally, physically and emotionally strong person to thrive under the enormous pressure and challenge that the Pragmatist expects and demands of followers, and to withstand the tough feedback this leader tends to deliver. People who are prone to burnout stand a poor chance of thriving under this leadership style.

Pragmatists must ensure that potential followers have the psychological reserves to enthusiastically attack those audacious goals and personal growth. It's important to stay vigilant for the warning signs of burnout, such as excessive cynicism, low energy, irritability (especially with customers), disillusionment, low self-esteem and hopelessness.

I've strolled through offices where these warning signs appear ubiquitous. The first step to tackling burnout is tracking the history of how it developed. Think back to a time during which people were happy and fulfilled. When did the signs of burnout first emerge? What was happening at that time that may have triggered the physical, emotional and/or mental exhaustion? It may take days or weeks to uncover the roots of burnout, but it's typically worth the effort to avoid overwhelming employees with a Pragmatist onrush.

Always remember that working for Pragmatists can be burnout-inducing. Erika Nardini, CEO, Barstool Sports, a satirical sports and men's lifestyle blog, said as much in a recent interview:

> I think I'm punishing. I have a large ability to grind. If
> I want something or if I believe in something or I think

something should be done better, I will push and push until I exhaust people. I really value stamina and drive. I am bad with stagnation and complacency. It's not just about winning, but did we do everything possible to make something happen?

Even about their hiring process, Erika says bluntly:

...If you're in the process of interviewing with us, I'll text you about something at 9 pm or 11 am on a Sunday just to see how fast you'll respond. The right response time is "within three hours." It's not that I'm going to bug you all weekend if you work for me, but I want you to be responsive. I think about work all the time, but I want people who are also thinking.[13]

The Leader Is Not Following in the Footsteps of a Legendary Pragmatist

There is one final context that bears mentioning; it is tough to successfully apply the Pragmatist leadership style when you're following in the footsteps of another Pragmatist, especially a very successful one.

The late Steve Jobs was a Pragmatist, but his successor, Tim Cook is not. The legendary Jack Welch, CEO of GE was a Pragmatist, but his successor Jeff Immelt was not. It is often the case that while people will achieve extraordinary results for the Pragmatist, the leader that follows has a doubly difficult challenge. First, it's tough to follow in the footsteps of a legend, regardless of their leadership style. Second, when that legend is a Pragmatist, there's a tendency for followers to think, "I gave that extraordinary effort when Steve Jobs yelled at me, but c'mon, he was Steve Jobs—genius, tireless worker, audacious goal-setter, etc. Are you as much of a genius as Steve was? Because if you're not, I'm unlikely to give you the same credence."

This doesn't mean that Steve's successor can't achieve similarly extraordinary results. Tim Cook's first years as CEO of Apple have been very successful. But achieving those results will generally require a different leadership style. Not only may employees have reached their limit under a Pragmatist, but the intense Pragmatist style commands such tremendous respect from followers that an immediate successor who attempts to adopt a similar style risks looking like a cheap imitation.

WARNING SIGNS THAT THE PRAGMATIST STYLE ISN'T WORKING

The Pragmatist leadership style can achieve amazing results, but it's critical not to push things too far, or you will risk losing the support of your followers. These five warning signs may indicate that the Pragmatist leadership style is coming across as too tough…

Warning Sign #1: You Walk into a Room and People Stop Talking

One of the surest signs that a Pragmatist has crossed the line from respect to fear is when they walk into a room and the chatter immediately turns to silence. Contrary to popular belief, this does not mean people were talking about you. But an abrupt shutdown of conversation is often a sign that people are afraid of you.

Remember back in high school when you had that really tough teacher whose entrance into the classroom caused every student to suddenly "zip it," for fear of getting yelled at or sent to the principal's office? If you enter a room and have flashbacks to that tough teacher, then you may have strayed from respected to feared.

We all like meetings to quickly come to order, and it's perfectly normal to not want your office to be a coffee klatch; however, there's a difference between a room quieting down when you enter versus people shutting up mid-sentence out of fear. Stay aware of this warning sign.

Warning Sign #2: When You Give Constructive Feedback, Employees Are Very Quiet

Every successful leader, regardless of their leadership style, is going to give tough feedback or constructive criticism. Ideally, the recipient of that feedback will have a response or ask questions. Maybe they ask for clarification. Or, perhaps they share their side of things. Occasionally, they might respectfully disagree. In a perfect world, they'll say something like, "Gee, you're right...I totally get it now." It tells a much different story when the recipient of constructive criticism sits there quietly, without much response. This is often an indicator that the person has entered mental shutdown, perhaps in an effort to survive a verbal beating.

When constructive feedback is given perfectly, the recipient has a "light bulb moment," where they realize the nature of their error, how the error occurred, and how to make things better next time. I call this "making a corrective leap." When delivered too harshly, constructive feedback can cause the recipient to get defensive, shut down mentally, and never make that "corrective leap." They fail to do anything positive or productive with the feedback.

If you observe the latter response happening often, with more than one of your employees, then you may need to dial down on the toughness and focus on delivering more "constructive" and less "criticism."

Warning Sign #3: You Do More than 60% of the Talking in Meetings

Occasionally when I am coaching a senior executive, I'll attend a few of their meetings. One of the metrics that I track during those meetings is how many minutes the executive speaks versus everyone else in the room. I literally use a stopwatch, just like an old-school gym teacher. If the executive does more than 60% of the talking, then it's a pretty good sign that their leadership style has gotten too tough.

There's a difference between a meeting and an assembly. In an assembly, it's perfectly legitimate to gather staff and deliver a presentation. If you've got a big announcement or a new policy change, then the largely one-way flow of information of assembly can be acceptable. Meetings are different. In a meeting, you brought those people into the room to solicit and gather their input, elicit their great ideas, and to avail yourself of their innovative thoughts. That won't happen if you're doing all of the talking.

Sometimes leaders dominate a meeting because they have trouble sitting quietly, whether from ego, ADHD or other cause. But another reason that leaders may do all the talking is because their employees are too afraid to open their mouths. This situation can cause a lot of trouble. Test this out in your next meeting. Stop talking for a few minutes. If your employees naturally pick up the conversation, then you're probably okay. But if there's an awkward lull, or people just stare, waiting for you to speak again, then you may have an issue that must be addressed.

Warning Sign #4: Your Employees Are Anxious
How can you tell if your employees are anxious? Well, you can ask them—but when employees think that their boss is too harsh, then they usually won't answer direct questions such as, "Are you feeling anxious right now?" Frankly, asking that question so bluntly has the potential to push people completely over the edge.

Instead, you've got to watch and listen to what your employees do and say. One indication of anxiety is when employees make mistakes and miss deadlines. People don't typically perform as well in panicked states as they do in a more relaxed frame of mind. Another sign is that when these folks make mistakes, they'll often beat themselves up, saying things like, "I just can't do this," or "I'll never finish in time," or "I'm going to get fired for sure!"

Catastrophizing is when people magnify an unpleasant situation into a life-and-death catastrophe, exaggerating a bad

situation into an intolerable one. Anxious employees are especially prone to catastrophizing. When you hear your people say words like "never" or "impossible" or "failure" or "can't," these are indications of catastrophizing, and thus, anxiety.

While your inclination may be to yell exhortations to "suck it up" and "stop whining," that's the wrong move. Instead, back off a little, break your project into smaller pieces so that people aren't so overwhelmed, and calm your voice. You don't have to invite everyone into the courtyard to join hands and sing folk songs. Just dial down your intensity by 20%. This will give employees a chance to regain their emotional footing, and once that happens, their performance will shoot back up.

Warning Sign #5: Your Employees Don't Bring You Bad News
Every company is going to have bad news. Whether the issues are big or small, balls will be dropped, customers will be disappointed, and deadlines will be missed. While you can't prevent bad things from happening, you can ensure that you know about them as soon as they occur.

Denying bad news doesn't make it go away. In fact, the opposite is true. Leaders who know what's going wrong in their operations generally have a higher career survival rate than those in denial. In order to know what's going wrong, your employees must be comfortable enough to walk into your office and say, "Boss, we've got a problem," before the problem becomes unmanageable. Pay attention to whether or not you get bad news, and how much. If the information flow is weak or nonexistent, then this may be a sign that your leadership style has become too harsh and that employees are terrified to walk into your office and speak the truth.

Soften things up a bit by asking employees about what's been getting in their way and how you can help fix it. This gentler version of "What's going wrong?" is much more apt to invite honest answers. And when employees do tell you about bad news, take extra pains to avoid any blame or anger. Show your gratitude for the insight you've just received by saying, "Thanks for sharing with me." This will go a long way towards helping employees feel safe bringing you bad news as it happens.

SHOULD YOU EVER TRY TO BECOME MORE OF A PRAGMATIST?

Even if Pragmatist isn't your default leadership style, there are times when you might consider employing several of the Pragmatist characteristics described heretofore.

Perhaps you're leading a team of smart, conscientious, motivated, emotionally healthy people, and yet, you're collectively falling short of your goals. Maybe your big project is behind deadline, you're missing budget numbers, or your competitors are consistently outpacing you. While there are other potential causes, the problem just might be that your folks are not facing sufficient challenges. There are specific signs that your team may need a bigger dose of the Pragmatist leadership style.

First, is everyone on your team still really happy, even though they are missing goals? Work should not be demoralizing—results are much better if it's not—but it can be problematic if everyone's mood is still upbeat while falling behind and getting trounced by the competition.

In the past few years, there have been a spate of books on how to be happy. Not deeply fulfilled, emotionally resilient, high achieving, or doing something truly meaningful and significant with your life, but rather, happy. In one of these happiness books, the author tells a story about a woman who loved reading literature so much that she decided to pursue her doctorate in the field. According to the story, the woman got into a good program and started taking classes, but before long she felt overwhelmed by the challenges. In the face of grades, deadlines, papers, rewards, punishments, etc., she lost her passion for reading.

The author of the book was making a totally different point in telling this story, but here is what I took away from it: Work is hard, and if you want to be great at something, maybe you want to crush your competitors or beat a deadline, then it's not always going to be fun. Think about a sport coach's reaction if their team is getting killed but the players are still having lots of fun on the field. Wouldn't the coach be angry, and deservedly so? Of course, and that's a sign that your team may need a bit more of the Pragmatist style, with a particular emphasis on pushing people to give maximal, 100% effort, and to take stock of their weaknesses and make improvements.

Another sign that you may want to try the Pragmatist style is when your team relies solely on consensus for making decisions, and, as a result, important decisions aren't made, or take far longer than they should. Let's take a look at what consensus actually means. According to Merriam-Webster, consensus means "a general agreement, unanimity, and group solidarity." In practice, most leaders define consensus as getting everyone in the room to agree. Just based on those definitions, it's easy to see the challenges of reaching a consensus.

Imagine that you convene a team to decide if you should raise or lower the price on your best product. You have employees and colleagues on the team who fall on both sides of the debate, and each camp is armed with equally persuasive data. In a situation such as this, reaching consensus could involve hours, or even days of discussion and debate. Non-stop arguments reverberate off the walls of the hot, cramped meeting space, and stacks of empty pizza boxes and coffee cups build in all four corners of the room. At some point, you may regret having convened this group, and in a fog of frustration, wonder if consensus is an unachievable fantasy. And, as you are not taking any action to change the price on your best product, there is a good chance that it is delivering your competitors a market opportunity.

Consensus doesn't have to be a bad thing; if it's your primary group decision-making format and works well for you, then don't change. But if you feel hamstrung by consensus, then you might need a bit more Directiveness. Walmart CEO Doug McMillon says that while top executives need to gather the collective wisdom of their teams, "waiting for consensus can kill you, because speed matters, too." Walmart's challenge, he says, "is to get the right few people in the room to make the best decision and get on with it."[14]

Let's assume that, after reading this section, you want to incorporate Pragmatist characteristics into your leadership repertoire. Where should you start? The following are four simple techniques for applying elements of the Pragmatist leadership style:

Pragmatist Technique #1: Bounded Consensus

Let's return to our team scenario where you're deciding whether to raise or lower prices on your best product. You're not going to employ consensus, because you want to try something a bit more in line with a Pragmatist, but you also don't want to dictate a decision to the team. Here's what you should do. At the beginning of your meeting, say the following:

> "The purpose of this meeting is to decide whether we should raise or lower our prices on Product X. I know that there are good ideas in all directions, so we're going to take the next 90 minutes and flesh out the pros and cons of each. Ideally, we'll start moving towards a general consensus, and maybe even achieve one. But in the event that we don't reach a full consensus, then I'll weigh all the options and make a decision using everyone's input. This ensures that we get everyone's best thinking, but also gives us an escape valve so we're not trapped in this room for eight hours straight."

I call this approach "bounded consensus." It's a sincere attempt at consensus, but it offers leaders and meeting participants a way out in the event that true consensus proves elusive. It also allows you to test a technique closer in style to the Pragmatist while still allowing for an attempt at consensus.

However, there is a caveat. If you're really not interested in consensus, or you've already made your decision, then don't feign interest in consensus. One of the things that makes consensus so powerful, is that you can end up with a decision no one anticipated. But if you're truly not open to that possibility, and there are times when you won't be, then don't waste everyone's time faking consensus. Focus instead on building buy-in for the decision you've already made.

Pragmatist Technique #2: Nominal Group Technique
Another technique for overcoming some of the drawbacks of consensus is the Nominal Group Technique. This easy approach to speed decision-making encourages the quieter people on your team to speak up (i.e., challenges them) and gives you more control over the louder voices on the team. All the technique requires is to exert, in Pragmatist fashion, a bit more Directiveness over the group.

Let's say the team has a decision to make. The meeting agenda that went out to everyone stated that the purpose of the meeting is to debate and decide on the proposal price for the new project being pitched to ACME Corp. You invited seven people to the meeting, and each of them brings a unique and valuable perspective to making this decision. Obviously, it's important to hear what each of them has to say.

As soon as everyone settles down, pass around sheets of paper, or if it's a virtual meeting, use a web meeting tool that allows people to write in responses. Then, give these directions:

"We're going to take five minutes now, and what I would like is to gather your individual ideas about how you think we should price this proposal. I want the number, but I also want to hear why you think it's the right number, so back it up with pros and cons, the whys and the why nots, etc. You have five minutes to write it down and then we're going to pass the papers forward to me to be discussed."

The Nominal Group Technique quickly and easily accomplishes three big things. First, it forces everyone to take a step back and actually do some thinking. This applies especially to those loud voices I mentioned earlier who often commandeer the meeting by shouting out the first idea that pops into their mind. Second, it gives every voice in the meeting an equal chance to be heard. And third, once everyone's ideas and thoughts are written down and collected, then you now have the opportunity to control the discussion that takes place in this meeting.

One way to accomplish this is to go through those responses one at a time and share what's written. The first submission might state, "I feel the contract should be priced at $12.5 million, which is $2.5 million higher than we usually charge for this job, but I support this higher number based on the tight timeline we're facing, which is going to mean more manpower diverted from other work, etc." Then you'll move on to the second response, which might say, "I think that $8.5 million is the right pricing for the job, which I acknowledge sounds pretty lowball, until you factor in the numbers I've provided below that outline the additional business that this new client will potentially bring our way." And you'll continue to read everyone's submission until you've reviewed everyone's ideas.

Another approach you can take to the Nominal Group Technique is to start the meeting by saying "I'm going to give every person here three minutes, with no interruptions from anyone, to share with the team your thoughts on how you think we should price this proposal and why." Just as in asking people to write it down, you immediately make everyone on the team more thoughtful. The people who might be inclined to shout out with kneejerk responses are forced to tone it down, and the folks who may be inclined to passively hang back are forced to stand up and say, "Here is what I'm thinking."

Whichever of these two approaches you take to the Nominal Group Technique, you will have effectively equalized the voices in the meeting and exerted more control over the group, which is a good starting point for trying out the Pragmatist style.

Pragmatist Technique #3: Difficult Goals

Almost everyone has set a goal or two in their life. Every year, more than 50% of people make New Year's Resolutions to lose weight, quit smoking, work out, save money, etc. A majority of employees working for large companies participate in some sort of annual corporate and individual goal-setting process. Virtually every corporate executive on earth has formal goals, scorecards, visions, etc. And who among us hasn't fantasized about having more money, a better body, more success at work, a swankier house, etc.? All of these are goals.

And yet, notwithstanding the ubiquity of goals, many of us never achieve our goals. And the goals we do achieve often fall far short of extraordinary.

One of my studies found that only 15% of people believed that their goals for this year were going to help them achieve great things. And only 13% thought that their goals would help them maximize their full potential. One of the big reasons why most goals are so ineffective is that they're not difficult enough.

Think about the most significant and meaningful accomplishments in your life. These can be either professional or personal achievements. For example: "When I started a new business," or

"The day I ran a marathon," or "Standing in the starting gate at the Olympics," or "That breakthrough product I invented," or "When I nursed my sick child back to health," or "When I got my college degree." It's no one's call but yours to name the victories that have been the most important to you.

Based on your responses, consider the following set of questions:

- Were those accomplishments easy or hard to achieve?
- Did I exert a little or a lot of effort?
- Did I already know everything I needed to know when I started out or did I have to learn new skills in order to succeed?
- Was I completely worry free or did I have a few doubts or even nervousness along the way?
- Was I totally relaxed throughout the process or did I get "amped up" (excited, alert, elevated heart rate, etc.)?

Personally, every noteworthy accomplishment I've ever achieved was difficult. It was hard to do, demanded a lot of effort, I had to learn new things, I had moments of worry, and I was totally amped up. I'm betting it's the same for you.

Now, think about the goals you typically set for your employees. Do you make those goals just as challenging as your big goals were, or do you set goals that are achievable and realistic? Far too many leaders pick the latter. In other words, they tell people to do the exact opposite of what they did with the difficult goals that they set for themselves that resulted in their amazing achievements.

About 40 years ago, two psychologists, Edwin Locke and Gary Latham, dramatically advanced the science of difficult goals. Their scientific studies involving more than 40,000 subjects provided conclusive validation that people who set or are given difficult goals achieve much greater performance levels than do people who set or are given weaker goals that send the message, "Just do your best."

In one of Gary Latham's experiments, drawn from his early work with Weyerhaeuser (the giant forestry, wood, paper company), the research team studied how difficult goals could improve the performance of logging truck drivers. For logging trucks, as with many commercial trucks, the goal is to load them as closely as possible to their maximum legal weight, to minimize the need for multiple runs, which costs time, fuel, trucks, etc. But, it's not easy to make happen; giant logs are many different sizes, they must be fit on the trucks, weights must be accurate, etc.

For this experiment, it was determined that a load that was 94% of the maximum legal net weight would be difficult, but not impossible to achieve. When workers were given a "do your best" goal, they loaded the trucks to approximately 60% of the maximum legal weight, resulting in a huge amount of wasted space. But, when they were given the significantly more difficult goal of loading the trucks to 94% of their maximum legal weight, lo and behold, that's exactly what happened. By the way, not only did the workers exceed all expectations, but this one simple experiment, conducted in Oklahoma, actually saved the company around $250,000.

It doesn't much matter what the situation is; setting difficult goals leads to better performance. Difficult goals work because they force us to pay attention; we can't simply sleepwalk through them. Maybe they arouse our attention because they're a little scary, or really exciting, or they're just a big departure from our normal daily routine. But whatever the reason, difficult goals get our brains worked up. And that's where you're going to get great performance.

Here's how to start. First, ask your followers, "What are you going to learn from this goal?" You want to hear how this goal will stretch your employees and what skills they'll have to learn to achieve this goal. An appropriately difficult goal, a goal that puts one right in that sweet spot of challenge, is going to require your people to learn. It's going to stretch their brains, excite neurons, amp them up and awaken their senses. If someone can breeze through a goal without learning, then it's just not difficult enough. So how much learning is enough learning? Well, ask your employees to think about their greatest personal accomplishments and use that as your measuring stick. They need to be learning about that much for every goal. Another way to think about it is that a goal has the optimal level of difficulty when it requires two to four major new learning experiences.

What if a goal isn't going to generate that level of learning and growth? That's a sign that you need to make the goal about 20% more difficult, which is usually enough to get the brain excited and start those neurons firing.

As a second step, ask your employees to answer this question: "To what extent is this goal within my comfort zone?" And then give them the following five choices as a response:

1. Totally within my comfort zone ("Don't worry, I can do this with my eyes closed!")
2. Pretty much within my comfort zone ("I'm awake, but hardly in a state of excitement.")
3. A little outside of my comfort zone ("I feel a little twinge of excitement or nervousness.")
4. Outside of my comfort zone ("I'm on pins and needles and totally alert. You've got my full attention!")
5. So far outside of my comfort zone that I'm too dumbfounded to even respond ("I'm in such a terror-stricken state that I can't even reply!")

This test is pretty subjective and requires a personal judgment call, but the most effective goals are going to be somewhere around number 4. Numbers 1 and 2 are way too easy and number 5 is way too hard. But number 3 is getting close and number 4 is right on the money.

If your employees answered the above question with number 1 or 2, it's a sign that you should make your goal another 20% more difficult. If they answered with number 5, make it 20% less difficult.

Pragmatist Technique #4: On-the-Job Learning

Employees who score high on survey questions such as, "I will have to learn new skills to achieve my assigned goals for this year," have higher scores on questions such as:

- "I consider myself a high performer."
- "The work I do makes a difference in people's lives."
- "I recommend this company to others as a great place for people to work."
- "I recommend my boss to others as a great person to work for."

Unfortunately, my research shows that only 42% of workers say they "Always" or "Frequently" learn on the job, while another 39% say they "Never" or "Rarely" learn on the job.[15]

The good news is that, with a dose of the Pragmatist style, you can correct this for your employees. Holding monthly conversations where you ask employees the following two questions will encourage and ensure new learning. Keeping notes to record the results of these conversations will help in tracking employee progress.

On-the-Job-Learning Question #1: What things would you like to get better at this next month?

This goal-focused question lets employees know that you want them to grow and that there are cool things on the horizon that they can learn. But it also establishes the expectation that learning, growth and development are job requirements.

31

On-the-Job-Learning Question #2: What things are you better at now than you were last month?
Setting challenging goals is a great way to enforce learning, but if people don't realize or can't verbalize what they've learned, then the experience falls flat. Formal training programs are a great means of new learning, but so are the subtler, on-the-job learning experiences that often go unnoticed. This question nudges employees to recall all of the learning they have experienced, such as learning new negotiating skills or improving time management practices.

WHAT TYPES OF EMPLOYEES DO AND DON'T WORK WELL WITH THE PRAGMATIST

Chris Paul is an NBA point guard, he's with the Houston Rockets as I write this, and an assured future Hall of Famer. But he's achieved recognition not just for his remarkable on-court skills, but also for what can most nicely be described as "competitive fire." According to a recent profile on ESPN,[16] a former teammate, David West, summed up Chris as, "hell-bent on winning."

Jamal Crawford, another former teammate, said in the same profile that he had never encountered such a blunt, barking leader as Paul. "It was almost like a shock, like, 'Whoa!' The thing I had to learn about him is that he's very in-your-face, but it's only for the betterment of the team. It's not to embarrass you. It's not for anything else other than the team to be successful. He has no agendas. He has no hidden anything. Once I understood that [during] the first ten games our first year playing together, I was like, 'Oh, it's not how he says it, it's the message.' He's always talking, always communicating. For that, I think it was great for me, personally. I can't speak for everybody else."

Jamal's statement, "I think it was great for me, personally. I can't speak for everybody else." perfectly encapsulates an important, and perhaps revolutionary, idea: Not every personality responds equally well to each of the four leadership styles. Some employees have the ideal character makeup to survive and thrive under the leadership of the hard-charging Pragmatist. For others, however, following the Pragmatist leader results immediately in disengagement and a search for the nearest exit.

My research has discovered several characteristics that positively, and sometimes negatively, correlate with idealizing the Pragmatist leadership style. We discovered these characteristics by assessing and analyzing the personality characteristics of employees and then measuring how they respond to the Pragmatist leadership style. Here's what I found:

People who respond well to the Pragmatist style tend to say that being average in their work is a truly terrible thing. Obviously, given the audacious goals and maximal effort so typical of the Pragmatist, this makes perfect sense. When the Pragmatist exhorts followers to aim higher, move faster, and make a dent in the universe, they're clearly implying that being average is not okay—and their most enthusiastic followers feel the same way.

Similarly, a person who is always pushing to do things bigger, better and faster will also tend to respond more positively to the Pragmatist. The same applies to people who set career or business goals that others describe as difficult or audacious, and who would rather take on a goal that is challenging and difficult, as opposed to one at which they feel confident. Those with a history of demanding more from their careers and themselves are not likely to find the demanding style of the Pragmatist particularly shocking. In fact, they're more apt to idealize the Pragmatist, because they see in their leader characteristics that they ostensibly desire in themselves.

There is also a competitive aspect to the Pragmatist's successful followers. For example, someone who declares that they work to get ahead in life and outperform others, or who enjoys showing off their abilities and impressing others, will tend to thrive when following the Pragmatist leader.

Success typically entails at least some competition. Whether it's because most readers of this book live in primarily capitalist and meritocratic societies in which competition is an immutable reality, or because competition is actively sought as motivational fuel, one is unlikely to climb to the highest rungs of success without encountering competition. Of course, not everyone enjoys competition or views it positively, and these people will be less inclined to follow the Pragmatist leader.

It has been said that Pragmatist leaders don't suffer fools gladly. Well, it turns out, neither do their followers. The person who admits that they feel strong annoyance and irritation towards people whom they consider lacking in intelligence, or who are "wrong," whether it applies to a belief, practice or standard, may enjoy working for the Pragmatist. So too will the person who acknowledges that they hold grudges. Does this mean that everyone who likes working for the Pragmatist is mean-spirited and angry? Not at all. It just indicates that competitive, driven people can become irritable when dealing with someone they view as an impediment or even a saboteur. And, they're less apt to paint a fake smile on their face to camouflage that irritation.

My research also discovered that those who idealize the Pragmatist leadership style tend to have an analytical bent, be highly detail-oriented, believe in "dotting the i's and crossing the t's," and use careful, detailed analyses to make decisions. While it's certainly possible to be a nonlinear thinker and gut-feeling decision-maker and still respond well to a Pragmatist leader, given the characteristics I've detailed, it's not terribly surprising that the analytical types fare better. Nor is it surprising that people who flourish in environments with rules and detailed processes are also more likely to prefer working for the Pragmatist.

CHAPTER 2
THE DIPLOMAT

Sheldon Yellen is the CEO of BELFOR Holdings, Inc., a billion-dollar disaster relief and property restoration company. He's a successful CEO, and one of the things that makes him truly notable is that every year he handwrites a birthday card to each of the company's nearly eight thousand employees. Yes, you read that correctly. Yellon doesn't outsource this activity to his assistant. Since he started writing cards over three decades ago, it has been his project entirely.

Speaking of his assistant, when Business Insider spoke to Gail Kennedy, who has worked with Yellen for more than two decades, she had this to say about her boss and his heartfelt commitment to writing the cards:

> Since I started working at BELFOR 21 years ago, I have always looked forward to receiving a birthday card from Sheldon and I think I have saved nearly every single card. It really is an amazing tradition for a company of our size. The cards always include a personalized note or memory shared, demonstrating how much Sheldon personally cares about every employee.[1]

Yellen tells it like this: "People say to me all the time that the customer comes first. But I'll say, 'I'm sorry, but my people come first.' And I truly believe that."[2] Yellen's got to believe it, otherwise handwriting nearly eight thousand birthday cards a year seems like utter madness. But when it comes to caring about his people, he's the real deal, saying, "When leaders forget about the human element, they're holding back their companies and limiting the success of others. Focusing only on profit and forgetting that a company's most important asset is its people will ultimately stifle a company's growth."[3]

Yellen is also unique in other ways that he communicates with employees. He still uses a flip phone instead of a smartphone, because, as he explains, "You can't show and feel emotion, compassion, passion or intent through a smartphone, through text." Having a flip phone encourages conversations, and Yellen wants to talk to his employees, whom he considers his family. "I want people to talk to me," he says, "I want them to hear my passion. If someone has something to say to me, they know they can pick up the phone. I'll answer their question. I am approachable."[4]

THE DIPLOMAT STYLE DEFINED

Diplomats rate high in Feeling and much lower in Structure, Directiveness, and Challenge. Overall, when we chart Diplomats' scores on these four factors, they look something like the following (the bars represent the range of scores for each of the factors with the lines inside the bars representing where the majority of scores fall):

Rating high on Feeling means that the Diplomat regularly asks employees about their motivators and demotivators. The Diplomat cares deeply about the personal needs of employees, wants to create an environment in which employees genuinely like one another, and is especially concerned that employees find their work personally fulfilling. Pushing employees to develop their weaknesses

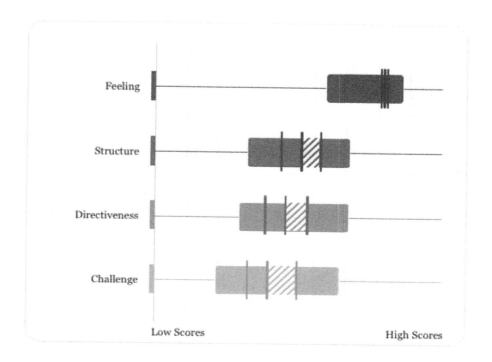

Low Scores   High Scores

or to give maximal, 100% effort is not a priority, nor is requiring final decision-making authority or having full control over how employees perform their work. Sending a handwritten birthday card to every employee, such as Sheldon Yellen does, would be well in the ballpark for a Diplomat, but you won't find the Diplomat hammering employees with formal procedures, rules and policies.

Diplomats prize interpersonal harmony, the social glue and affiliative force that holds groups together. They tend to be kind, social and giving. They enjoy building deep personal bonds with their employees, have a talent for avoiding conflict, and, when conflict does present, they are gifted mediators who can quickly reach a resolution.

Occasionally, other leadership styles will refer to Diplomats as "touchy-feely," insinuating that the Diplomat's people-first mind-set somehow renders them less effective and can even predict poor financial performance. There is plenty of evidence to the contrary. In 2016, for example, when Business Insider profiled Shigenobu Nagamori, the billionaire CEO of electric motor manufacturer Nidec Corp., they titled the piece "This billionaire CEO cares about his employees more than investors, and the company's stock is up 457% since 2008."

In the article, Nagamori says "When I'm asked by investors, I tell them they're No. 1, but it's not what I really think. I speak my mind if shareholders ask strange questions at the annual general meeting. I tell them it would be better if the likes of you didn't own our shares. I say I can't choose my shareholders, but you can choose the company you invest in."[5]

And it's not just talk. As long as an employee is putting in the hours and effort, Nagamori is unwilling to fire them if they are lacking in talent. Instead, he seeks to find another position where the employee might perform better. Looking after employees, Nagamori says, is key to a company's success.[6] Perhaps this is why he regularly sits down to meals with his staff.

Another success story is Scott Scherr, founder, President and CEO of Ultimate Software, a provider of cloud-based human capital management solutions. Employee perks at Ultimate include free meals, monthly ice cream truck visits, on-site massages, acupuncture and cupping, yoga, Pilates, and exercise boot camps. For the third consecutive year, Ultimate ranked number one on Fortune magazine's "Best Workplace in Technology" list for 2018, and you'll find numerous positive Glassdoor reviews from Ultimate employees including, "Commitment to putting employees first is very real and evident daily," and, "They put their people first in all areas, they truly care about the employees and they don't just say it, they walk the talk." All of this so called "touchy-feely" doesn't seem to be getting in the way of the company's success. Ultimate Software was named to Forbes list of 25 fastest-growing public companies in tech in 2017 after showing three years of strong, profitable growth, combined with industry-leading projected earnings growth for the next three to five years.

Scherr, who was recently named one of America's favorite CEOs by Forbes, had this to say about maintaining a company culture that puts people first: "Just take good care of your employees. I don't know any other way to do business...take good care of your people always—no matter what is going on outside of your business—and they will take care of your customers. That's the reason for our 26 years of growth and our financial performance."[7]

Working for Diplomats is fun and social, far more so than working for other leaders, especially hard-charging Pragmatists. But it's more than just ice cream and yoga. Diplomats genuinely want to keep their people from feeling uncomfortable or anxious. This means that instead of putting the emphasis on challenging their people, they focus on putting their people in positions that leverage their strengths. Or, in the words of Dr. King Owyang, CEO of Computime, "You have to be able to make use of [employees'] strengths and complement their weaknesses. Most of the time, people do not fully understand where their strengths and weaknesses lie. Leaders have to help them recognize that. If you can do that, that's half the battle."[8]

As you might expect, traditional measures of employee satisfaction are often very high for Diplomats. For the appropriate people, working for the Diplomat is a great situation. The Diplomat is the most common of all the leadership styles. It's interesting to note that, unlike the Pragmatists, top-level executives have a lower percentage of Diplomats than other groups, such as Managers, Directors and Vice Presidents.

STRENGTHS AND WHERE THE DIPLOMAT STYLE WORKS BEST

All leadership styles work better in some contexts than in others. For example, the kind-hearted Diplomat might not be the ideal style to lead a company teetering on the brink of financial collapse, and that must quickly conduct mass layoffs. Not only might the Diplomat move too slowly while they take extra pains to reduce hurt and anxiety, but they're unlikely to perform well awash in so much stress.

However, there are many contexts in which the Diplomat does shine, including when:

- Retaining and engaging people are your top priorities.
- Your employees are hurting.
- Your employees need to know that someone cares.
- High performers are less engaged than everyone else.
- Job advancement and enrichment are limited.
- People want a fun, social place to work.
- Your top priority is maintaining exceptional results.
- You're following in the steps of a legendary leader.

Let's look at each of these situations in more detail...

Retaining and Engaging People Are Your Top Priorities
I heard Mark Cuban, who is not a Diplomat, speak a few years ago, and he was asked what management advice he would give to Facebook CEO Mark Zuckerberg. His answer was essentially that Facebook already has a killer business model, so Zuckerberg's number one priority should be retaining his über-talented employees and keeping them happy.

I found Cuban's answer somewhat striking, given that he operates more like a Pragmatist. After all, this is the same guy who also said, "I micromanage you until I trust you," and "Relaxing is for the other guy," and "Work like there is someone working 24 hours a day to take it all away from you."[9] But while it may seem somewhat out of character for Cuban to advocate adopting more of a Diplomat approach, he was absolutely correct.

For companies with killer business models, a top priority should be to engage and retain the people who execute that business model. The Pragmatist leadership style may have been what led the company to reach some audacious goals, but once those goals come to fruition, then the business must prioritize retaining its best people. Of course, the best way to keep those great people just might be to set audacious goals and provide ample learning opportunities; but of all the leadership styles, the Diplomat is often best positioned to execute that strategy.

The Diplomat knows that asking employees about their motivators and demotivators is the most accurate way to learn what kind of workplace engages them. Remember, the Diplomat cares deeply about the personal needs of employees, desires an environment in which employees genuinely like one another, and is very concerned that employees find their work personally fulfilling. Not every employee prioritizes working in a collegial, friendly, caring culture; some people really don't care about liking their coworkers. They want only to hit big goals and leave their friends outside of the office. But even in those situations, the Diplomat can still deliver great value, because this is the leader most likely to ask employees what impels them to leave or attracts them to stay.

A few years ago, a consulting company that was careening towards collapse called me in to assist. This firm had already churned through multiple CEOs, was bleeding cash and, perhaps most importantly, was losing its best employees. When the best people leave a consulting firm, clients tend to leave with them.

When they installed a new CEO, she determined that her first course of action needed to be retaining the company's top talent, and she channeled her inner Diplomat to meet this goal. Her first month's calendar was chock-full of interviews with employees. As she met with individual employees, she asked them to share their motivators and demotivators, and what they found personally fulfilling about their work. This CEO figured, correctly, that if she could stop people from quitting, then she would have ample time to set audacious goals, fix the operations and create interesting growth opportunities (i.e., utilize the Pragmatist, Steward and Idealist leadership styles). But in her people-intensive business, she knew that the company would not succeed if good employees (and their clients) kept leaving.

Your company or team needn't be on the verge of calamity to prioritize employee retention and engagement. The following two major indicators, both of which fall short of crisis, are excellent reasons to make securing employee retention and engagement top priorities.

Retaining and Engaging Indicator #1: Low Employee Engagement Scores

Studies pointing to a worldwide decline in employee engagement abound. Approximately half of employees are looking to leave their current jobs and only a quarter of employees are highly engaged. Regardless of whose studies you use, and there are plenty to choose from, everyone finds essentially the same thing—lots of employees do not love their jobs. The good news is, if you've got access to regular employee engagement survey data, then you can precisely track engagement and pinpoint which areas are suffering, and where you need to intervene as a Diplomat. But as you do so, heed my warning: don't be a "fake Diplomat."

I recently conducted a survey of 3,000 HR executives, and one of the survey questions asked, "How have your employee engagement survey scores changed over the past two years?" Survey participants were given the following four choices from which to select a response:

1. I don't know because we haven't surveyed regularly.
2. Our survey scores haven't changed significantly.

3. Our survey scores have declined.
4. Our survey scores were low, but they've improved dramatically OR they were high and they've stayed high.

Obviously, only No. 4 represents a good outcome. Frighteningly, only 22% of executives chose that option. Meanwhile, 13% of executives responded that their scores declined and 34% of companies responded that they do not regularly survey.

If you conduct an employee engagement survey and your scores decline, then that's not good. Perhaps there were extenuating circumstances, e.g., your company initiated layoffs or was acquired. While it's never ideal to see employee engagement decline, we might give a company in those types of situations a pass for a year or two. But not every one of the 13% of companies with declining scores experienced a disruptive event or set of circumstances.

One of the major reasons that employee engagement survey scores decline is that leaders conduct an employee engagement survey, but never act on the results. These leaders are what I call "fake Diplomats." They go through the motions that they associate with being a Diplomat, such as asking employees how they feel, but then they drop the ball by failing to do anything productive with the information gathered. Just imagine how it feels to be an employee in that situation; your bosses ask for your opinion, but when you give it, it is ignored. It provides a very short path to reducing whatever goodwill had been previously built and, frankly, leaders who are "fake Diplomats" generate far worse results than leaders with no Diplomat tendencies whatsoever.

As for the 34% of companies that don't survey employees regularly, it's not necessarily bad practice. If all signs point to a highly engaged workforce, and your Pragmatist, Steward or Idealist styles are working well, then a survey may be a waste of time and money. However, many of the companies that don't conduct employee engagement surveys aren't avoiding the exercise because of time constraints or tight budgets; they're avoiding the survey because they are afraid of the answers.

I know that facing the truth and the unknown can be frightening; it's why so many people avoid life-saving medical exams. In some cases, it's because those exams are uncomfortable, but it is often because learning the results of a medical exam is potentially scary. Years ago, a dentist asked me if I wanted an inexpensive screen for oral cancer; it was twenty-five dollars and required only a quick cheek swab. I did have the test, but I initially hesitated, because all I could think was, "How am I going to get through the rest of my day if I discover that I've got oral cancer?" The lesson is simple; you might not love the results you get when you start regularly conducting employee engagement surveys, but think of how great it will feel, for you and your employees, when you uncover easily corrected issues.

Retaining and Engaging Indicator #2: Negative Online Company Reviews

Another reason for leaders to prioritize employee retention and engagement is that poor employee reviews, readily accessible on job sites such as Glassdoor, Great Place to Work and Indeed, make it more difficult to attract new talent. Glassdoor's recent stats show the site has nearly 38 million reviews and insights for more than 740,000 companies. According to a 2016 Glassdoor U.S. Site Survey, the majority of job candidates read six reviews before forming an opinion about a company and 70% of jobseekers now check reviews before they make career decisions.[10]

I recently spent five minutes on Glassdoor looking at the reviews for a large company that I selected at random. Some examples:

- Culture of senior management is bipolar. What is presented to the external world is not the harsh reality internally.
- Current climate is caustic. Fear is rampant.

- Tons of bureaucracy, processes, impediments to speed and efficiency.
- Too many hour-tracking tools for employees reflect clear micro management by the senior management.
- Spend too much time with internal processes. Not enough focus or time for our client objectives and needs.
- Too siloed, cannibalistic, no sense of a team. I was there for 3+ years and did not get to meet the full team.

Many companies are bound to have disengaged, or even disgruntled, employees. But in this age of online reviews, everyone's a critic, and it doesn't take thousands of negative reviews to impact your ability to attract new talent. Maybe you're a Pragmatist leader who needs ambitious and resilient followers to make a "dent in the universe." But if your potentially, high-performing candidates are reading negative reviews about your company, similar to those above, then your recruiters' jobs will be much more difficult. Negative online reviews are clear indicators that it's time to make employee retention and engagement top priorities.

Your Employees Are Hurting
The US presidential election in 2017 was one of the most vitriolic in the country's history, replete with misogyny, racism, and xenophobia. Following this unusually nasty contest, some CEOs saw that their employees were hurt, scared and scarred. In response, they smartly adopted a Diplomat leadership style as a first step in the healing process. One of the best examples of this pivot to Diplomat came from Jeff Weiner, CEO of LinkedIn, who sent an email message to employees immediately after the election. The email stated, in part (the emphasis in boldface is mine):

I spent much of yesterday talking with employees and leaders throughout LinkedIn about the U.S. election results and what it means to them personally and for us as a company. I wanted to briefly share what I heard and the implications for us going forward.

As might be expected from this long and sometimes brutal election cycle, **the emotional responses people expressed ran from shock and sadness to grief and mourning; some telling stories of celebratory outreach from colleagues; and yet others feeling nothing at all.** I heard women driven to tears of frustration over the fact a highly qualified woman was passed over once again for a leadership role, and saw men choke up as they recounted their stories; was told of how a highly talented and deserving co-worker, here from another country on an H1-B visa, was filled with dread over whether he and his family will have the opportunity to remain in the U.S.; and saw tears of joy from a mother recounting how her young son stood up in class, boasting how proud he was that his mom had voted.

Let's make sure to provide one another the time to process everything that's just transpired. As leaders and achievers, many of us have a natural tendency to solve other people's problems as soon as we hear them. However, we need to be sensitive to the fact that some members of the team don't need or even want immediate resolution. They don't want to hear rationalizations or participate in endless debates about why this unfolded the way that it did. **They may just want someone to listen.**

Others are ready to engage; to share their fears and anger, their hopes and dreams. **It's imperative to the healing process that we create a space where every individual at the company can feel safe when doing so; that everyone feels heard; and above all else, that every single employee of LinkedIn feels as if they truly belong here.** This dynamic must transcend race, religion, gender, creed, and country of origin. While we have always aspired to make this the case, it will be more important than ever given the misogynistic, racist, and xenophobic language heard at times throughout this election. That language and behavior has not and never will have a place at LinkedIn and we will continue to do everything within our power to create a safe and productive work environment for all of our employees.[11]

In his email, Jeff Weiner, who earned a slot on Glassdoor's 2017 list of the highest-rated CEOs in the world, describes how he spent most of the day listening to LinkedIn employees who were personally affected by the election results and pronounces his intent to create a space where everyone feels heard and safe. I added the bolding to emphasize the empathic, emotional, and caring language he uses. This email is a great illustration of the Diplomat leadership style in action, especially in times of anxiety and hurt.

Your Employees Need to Know that Someone Cares

In mid-2017, American Airlines announced a pay raise for pilots and flight attendants that would bring their pay in line with competitors Delta and United. At the time, American's pilots were paid about 8% less than Delta and United while flight attendants were paid about 4% less. In a letter to employees from American's CEO, Doug Parker, and President, Robert Isom, the pay issue was addressed as follows: this pay raise was "not about buying trust because we all know trust cannot be purchased...[this] is about doing the right thing."[12]

American Airlines is a big company, so this increase didn't come cheap. The airline estimated it would cost $230 million in 2017 and $350 million annually in 2018 and 2019. It is a lot, but, for a company with roughly $40 billion in revenue, it's probably not the end of the world.

That is not, however, how Wall Street saw it. American's stock dropped about 5% when the pay raise news was announced. Morgan Stanley downgraded American's shares and Citi analyst Kevin Crissey wrote, "This is frustrating. Labor is being paid first again. Shareholders get leftovers."[13]

Imagine for a moment that you're an employee at American and you're in the middle of all this. The owners of the company, the shareholders, have basically said that you're not worth a raise, that you're not worth being paid commensurate with your competitors, and that it's horrible that labor is being paid. Yes, it's fine if a failed CEO collects hundreds of millions for selling off the company to a big buyer, but American's roughly 40,000 pilots and flight attendants can't split $230 million? This sends a stunning message to employees.

There's an important lesson here about when you might want to apply Diplomat leadership. In this situation, Wall Street let it slip that they don't think employees are worth very much. And if the "ostensible owners" of the company don't value their workers, then the only people left who could, and should, value the workers, are the company's leaders.

High Performers Are Less Engaged than Everyone Else

Sometimes the need for a Diplomat's touch is limited to a particular group of employees, your high performers. In 2013, I published a study with findings so counterintuitive that it captured media attention all the way from NPR to *Forbes* to political talk radio. The study results showed that in nearly half of companies, low performers are happier than high performers.[14] This news was shocking because it's not how things are supposed to work. If you're a high performer, then you're supposed to be engaged and fulfilled. And if you're a low performer, you're expected to be miserable and disengaged. But that's not always the reality.

Imagine that it's Friday afternoon at 4 p.m., and you've got a major report due on Monday at 9 a.m. This report could make or break your career, and you're going to need help getting it done. You and whoever helps you can expect a long weekend of hard work, but a deadline is a deadline. To whom are you going to turn for help: the employee who gives 100% effort or the employee who gives 50% effort? Of course, you enlist the 100% high performer. And when the same situation occurs again next Friday, who do you think gets called on to make the painful sacrifice? Once again, it's a high performer. And it's the high performer who will get the call the weekend after that, and so on.

Who has the worst job on your team? The high performer does, and it can seriously impact engagement. When the Wall Street Journal covered my study, the story received over 200 online reader comments on the first day of publication. The following is one of those comments, and it reflects the sentiment of many of the others. "Things got so bad here we asked for a review from our corporate office HR department. They came and listened to our complaints and the lazy unproductive people had nothing bad to say. The productive hard workers had plenty to say and we asked to start making everyone accountable. It seemed like an easy request. Wrong. They did nothing. So the slackers are still slacking."

Those corporate office folks who came and listened to the frustrated employees were clearly "fake Diplomats;" they asked employees how they were feeling, but then didn't act on the feedback. When there is a group of people who are burned out, frustrated, disengaged, etc., then it's a good time to employ some true Diplomat skills. This means not just listening, but taking concrete action to ease the pain and frustration.

Job Advancement and Enrichment Are Limited
The Diplomat style isn't applied only for healing emotional wounds. It can also be a great leadership style when employees'

jobs aren't especially intrinsically stimulating, when there's limited opportunity for advancement, or when growth experiences are minimal. This can be impolitic to say, but some jobs are not particularly stimulating or even desirable. Take the job of filling out forms, for example. Even though it is necessary work, it's often not intellectually stimulating. Let's imagine that you manage people who perform this task, and you have no control over changing the makeup of their work; creative techniques such as job-crafting or enrichment are not possible. And yet, you're still held accountable to retain and engage your people.

This is where the Diplomat leadership style can be helpful. Maybe you can't offer many learning opportunities or promotions, but you can create an environment filled with positive reinforcement and warm relationships amongst the team. I've seen leaders overcome the limitations of boring jobs with everything from team happy hours to cupcake Fridays to deep conversations in which the leader helps employees prepare for their career after leaving the current job. And those are tasks typically best performed by the Diplomat leadership style.

People Want a Fun, Social Place to Work

Similar to the situation above, in 2017, the *Wall Street Journal* published an article called "New Jersey Has a Millennials Problem" which reported, "The state's employers are pushing landlords to remodel office spaces with cool perks to attract younger workers."[15] In brief, New Jersey is losing Millennials; more have left the state than have moved to the state. As a result, real estate developers are redoing office buildings to better attract younger workers.

For example, because Millennials have only recently moved away from their previous homes, the college campuses, the thinking goes that they're still accustomed to, and desire having social and recreational areas at their disposal. Real estate developers are now trying to recreate that college campus type of environment for companies. According to the article, "one example is the Warren Corporate Center, a property in Warren, N.J., owned as part of a joint venture with Rubenstein Partners. The partnership is building a stand-alone amenity building in the center of the 820,000 square-foot complex, featuring an indoor basketball court, conference room facilities, a food court with a coffee bar, fitness center, and a green roof with event space."[16]

Now, all those physical upgrades are lovely, but they won't be worth much if they're not supported by the appropriate leadership style. For example, imagine that the leader said to employees, "Sure, you've got a basketball court, but we're here to work, not have fun, plus I like when you all compete with each other, not do a bunch of sports-related teambuilding." A company can have all of the basketball courts and coffee bars in the world, but with a leader who does not recognize the value of the amenities, they would only serve as a reminder of what employees are missing, and they are likely to be a pretty big demotivator. If you're in a world where competing for talent means offering a social experience, then you're likely best served by pairing those experiences with a Diplomat leadership style.

Your Top Priority Is Maintaining Exceptional Results

Disney has had its share of success. Their mission is crystal clear, and the talented people who choose to work there are typically filled with a deep sense of purpose for, and pride in, their work. So, much like Mark Zuckerberg's challenge of keeping all those smart people happy, Disney CEO Bob Iger faces a similar task. That's why, on the eve of the release of *Star Wars: The Force Awakens*, he sent a memo to all Disney employees that read, in part (once again the emphasis in bold is mine):

> "...we're now on the eve of releasing *Star Wars: The Force Awakens*, one of the proudest and most exciting moments in our Company's history.

It's been thrilling to see the remarkable level of team-work behind this effort—every single business unit across the Company has been part of launching this movie and building the future of this franchise, ensuring it will generate value for our Company for generations to come.

We often talk about our people as the Company's greatest strength and most valuable resource, because it's true. In a business like ours, driven by creativity and innovation, nothing is more important than the men and women who dream of new possibilities, set new standards of excellence, and create new opportunities, then work together to achieve them. And we're so fortunate to have thousands of cast members and employees around the world who accept the challenge and embody that spirit."[17]

Bob Iger is the CEO of a company whose talented people just created one of, if not the bestselling movies of all time. Should his top priority right now be to push employees harder, make their processes more disciplined, and get them to develop more skills? Or should his top priority be to care deeply about his employees' fulfillment, while keeping them feeling great and genuinely liking one another? I'd argue that given the success of their work product, his top priority is keeping those amazing people feeling great, so that they are eager to create an even more extraordinary work product for Disney.

You're Following in the Steps of a Legendary Leader
Sam Walton founded Wal-Mart, currently the world's largest company by revenue, and is deservedly an American business icon. But it's his successor, David Glass, whom I would like to highlight. Fortune Magazine wrote a great profile on Glass years ago that included the following (the emphasis in bold is mine):

Lost in the Wal-Mart lore is one of the great CEO success stories of recent times: the 12-year run of former chief David Glass. **Compared with his larger-than-life friend and mentor, Glass is low-key, without any outward evidence of ego or of the charisma of his predecessor.** But what he has achieved blows away anything taught in Harvard case studies. During Glass' tenure--from February 1988 to January 2000--the retailer's sales rose more than tenfold, to $165 billion; earnings soared to $5.4 billion from $628 million, and its stock price, adjusted for splits, moved from $3.42 a share to $55.[18]

We know that David Glass, while quiet and egoless, was an amazing CEO. He's an especially interesting study in the context of this chapter, because he also evidences the characteristics of a people-first Diplomat. When he was asked this question in the *Fortune* interview: "A lot of outsiders assume it must have been hard to follow Sam Walton. How did you manage your career in the shadow of a charismatic leader?" Glass responded:

> Most people have enough ego that they want to distinguish themselves from a charismatic leader, and that's what creates the problem. I've never had much ego, and I'm not worried about things like that. **I'm more interested in the satisfaction that we are doing the right things and we're getting it done and being a part of it. I like being part of a winning team. I don't have to be the winning team.**[19]

One of the hallmarks of Diplomats is their tendency to put the needs of others ahead of their own. This is why the Diplomat is often the right leader for the job when there is emotional strife, people are hurting, or they need to feel loved. Glass followed in the steps of a legend, Sam Walton, someone whom people both adored and mourned intensely. So how did he succeed following such a leader? Glass couldn't compete with Walton's charisma, but neither could he be utterly emotionless, especially with a grieving workforce. His best option, given the circumstances, was to care deeply about people, and support and cheer their success. The results speak for themselves.

WARNING SIGNS THAT THE DIPLOMAT STYLE ISN'T WORKING

Employing a Diplomat leadership style can deliver great results, but there are times when this style leader can go too far into the Diplomat realm, becoming too soft and yielding to be effective. Here are five warning signs that the Diplomat leadership style isn't working:

Diplomat Warning Sign #1: A Five-Minute Conversation Turns into Fifty Minutes

Imagine you give an employee a highly specific bit of constructive feedback, for example, "This report is too long. Tighten up the writing and shave off 1,000 words." This feedback should require no more of a response than "I got it, I'll fix it now." Now imagine that even though this feedback conversation should take only a few minutes, you find yourself engaged in a lengthy conversation with the employee about why they fell short, how it makes them feel, and why you're somehow to blame for their mistakes.

If this has ever happened to you, it's a warning sign that you've become too appeasing. It's good to encourage dialogue with your employees, and it's great when they feel comfortable sharing, but when employees believe they can talk themselves out of being criticized or held accountable, then that's a problem.

There are times when an employee just needs to say, "I'm sorry. I messed up. I'll fix it immediately." That's not indicative of a dictatorial environment; it's usually just a sign of an efficient and accountable operation. There are some conversations that should always be five minutes and done. If you regularly feel like five-minute conversations are turning into 50-minute therapy sessions, it's a strong sign that you've moved from approachable to acquiescent.

Diplomat Warning Sign #2: Your Meetings Get Off Topic and Take Too Long

Have you ever been in one of those meetings where one or more big personalities dominate the conversation? They talk louder than everyone else and all you can hear are their thoughts, their ideas, and their opinions. Quieter employees feel totally shut out from participating, so you miss their potentially valuable input. And when you try to rein in these big personalities, they manage to resist and keep on yakking and stealing the show.

Ideally, meetings are value-adding forums where all invitees participate. Isn't that why you called all of those people into the meeting in the first place? When you struggle to control the showboaters and loudmouths, and when these meeting disrupters don't respect your authority, formal or otherwise, it's a warning sign that you're being too soft and not forceful or commanding enough. Of course, people should talk; intense conversations can signal a healthy team. And you don't need to be overbearing about it, but you do need someone in the room with enough power to keep the conversation on track, on time, and thoroughly professional.

Diplomat Warning Sign #3: You Regularly Mediate Employee Conflicts Instead of Employees Solving Issues Themselves

It's troubling when a leader regularly gets sucked into employee conflicts. In an ideal world, employees nearly always act like adults and resolve conflicts themselves, reserving the boss-as-mediator for only the most serious issues. But in the real world, when a leader becomes too accommodating, employees quickly figure out that pleading their case to the boss will steer the boss to intervene on their behalf. It's quite similar to the games that kids play; whether it's "Ma, he's looking at me funny," or playing one parent off the other to get what they want.

When a leader has a no-nonsense, "suck-it-up" reputation, these manipulations are rare. But when the leader is seen as overly accommodating or appeasing, these games will be a frequent occurrence. If you find yourself regularly mediating employee conflicts instead of employees handling conflict themselves, take it as a warning sign that you may be overaccommodating your employees. Try dialing back your Diplomat style of leadership and see what happens.

Diplomat Warning Sign #4: The Same Problem Recurs Multiple Times

There isn't an organization on the planet that doesn't have employees who make mistakes; it's the price of doing business. However, when your employees continue to make the same mistakes, it's often a sign that they have not received the message that they need to improve. This is often the result of employees believing that their leader won't really follow through on enforcing consequences.

I'm not suggesting that leaders move to the opposite extreme, where employees are risk-averse and paralyzed by fear of being fired for a wrong move. That's every bit as damaging as being too soft. Rather, the effective leader will find the middle ground and communicate that "Mistakes are inevitable, but strive to avoid repeating the same mistake." Employees need to know that if they fail to take their mistakes seriously, and if they don't work diligently and earnestly to improve, that the consequences will be more than just their leader's expression of disappointment.

Diplomat Warning Sign #5: Employees Aren't Learning New Things

One of the biggest tests of leadership is: Are your people learning new things? If your answer is that they are not growing and developing, then it's a likely warning sign that your leadership style is too soft.

Ensuring that your people learn on the job isn't difficult. It simply requires sitting down with employees once a month and asking them, "What is something that you're better at now than you were last month?" If they don't have an answer, then follow up with questions to help them get on track. For example, you might ask, "What would you like to get better at this next month?" and, "What new skills are you going to have to develop this next year to reach your major goals?"

It's interesting that when you ask leaders, "Think about the most significant goals you've ever achieved in your life; were they easy or hard to achieve?" the answer is always "hard." Yet, in spite of this, those same leaders repeatedly set employee goals that are too easily achievable and realistic, and then wonder why there is no greatness. Give your people goals that challenge them, that push them outside of their comfort zone, and force them to learn new things. When employees are given difficult goals, it sends the message that their leader believes in them. In turn, they will believe in themselves and their capacity to grow and develop on the job.

SHOULD YOU EVER TRY TO BECOME MORE OF A DIPLOMAT?

Even if the Diplomat isn't your default leadership style, there are times when you might consider employing some of the Diplomat characteristics described heretofore.

Perhaps your best people are quitting, and you don't know why. Or maybe you've gone through some tough times and your employees are hurting. It could be that the jobs you're hiring for just aren't all that interesting, or your employees have just delivered the best product ever and now you're worried about keeping them happy and engaged. Any of these scenarios could signal a need for some Diplomat leadership style. So how do you actually adopt a Diplomat style? Here are three techniques to get you started...

Diplomat Technique #1: Shoves and Tugs

Here is one of the most important lessons about engaging your employees: everyone has Shoves and Tugs. Shoves are issues that demotivate you, drain your energy, stop you from putting forth maximum effort, and make you want to quit; they "shove" you out the door. Tugs are factors that motivate and fulfill you, make you want to deliver maximum effort, and keep you coming back every day; they "tug" at you to stay.

This seems simple enough, but here's the twist: Shoves and Tugs aren't flip sides of the same coin. Just because somebody has multiple Tugs during a week doesn't mean they don't have any Shoves. So, before you start trying to figure out how to provide people with meaningful Tugs, you've got to at least acknowledge, and ideally mitigate, their Shoves. If you don't, and those Shoves remain unaddressed, then employee engagement will take a dive.

Let me begin with an analogy that's unconventional, but that might help clarify this issue. Just as Shoves and Tugs are not opposites, neither are pain and pleasure. The opposite of pleasure isn't pain; it's just the absence of pleasure. Similarly, the opposite of pain isn't pleasure; it's just the absence of pain. If somebody is hitting my foot with a hammer, that's pain. When the hammering stops, it's not pleasure; there is just no more pain. If I'm getting the world's greatest back rub, that's pleasure. When it stops, it's not pain; it is simply no more pleasure.

Here's the lesson: If I'm getting a great back rub, it does not preclude someone from simultaneously hitting my foot with a hammer. If that happens, then the pain in my foot will totally detract from the pleasure I'm getting from the back rub. Here's a corollary lesson: If you walk past me one day and see that my foot is being hit with a hammer, then you cannot fix the pain in my foot by giving me a back rub. The only way to stop the pain in my foot is to stop the hammer from hitting it. And unfortunately, discovering those hammers has not typically been a goal of employee engagement surveys.

Every day, in organizations around the world, employees' feet are being hit with hammers, and their bosses' solution isn't to stop the hammer (i.e., eliminate the Shove), but rather to offer a back rub (i.e., offer a Tug). It's a big reason why half of employees are looking to leave their current jobs and only a quarter of employees are highly engaged.

Consider, for example, a software development team in Silicon Valley led by a manager named Chris. The department was on heavy deadline to finish a new product, and Chris' mounting anxiety was causing him to micromanage. He began instituting numerous "check in" meetings, widely acknowledged by the team as useless, and insisting on regular "no-work team lunch hours" that forced employees to work extra hours in order to stay on track to make the deadline.

Chris could feel the high emotional tension throughout the department, but rather than asking his team about the source of their frustration, he decided to take the team to Catalina Island for the weekend to relax. He figured it was a great way to offer a nice reward and get everyone's brains back into the game. When he made the announcement, more than a few of the programmers' heads nearly exploded. The last thing they wanted was more time with one other just hanging out and not working. They wanted to finish the project, hit the deadline, and go home to their families. They wanted to stop wasting time at work and just get the job done.

Chris made the mistake of trying to fix a Shove with a Tug, and it backfired. Yes, Catalina Island is beautiful, and perhaps in another circumstance it would have been a nice reward and a way to boost employee engagement. But, with his team already feeling the Shove of spending too much time away from the actual work of programming, not only was the Tug a poor choice, but Chris' credibility took a big blow for his insensitive lack of understanding as to what was really demoralizing his team.

When good employees must function in a Shove environment, such as dealing with low performers, stubborn roadblocks, or a terrible working environment, it's akin to being hit on the foot with a hammer multiple times. When you're suffering that level of pain, then Tugs, such as autonomy, the power to control an entire process, and the ability to work on innovative projects with great teams, aren't going to have a positive impact until you remove or reduce the frequency and severity of the Shoves.

The big lesson is that if you desire to improve employee engagement, then introducing Tugs alone will not work. Take the time to discover, acknowledge and, if possible, eliminate the Shoves. A Shoves and Tugs conversation doesn't have to be formal; in fact, it's actually better if it is not. The last thing you want is to make it seem like a performance appraisal. Get out from behind your desk and invite employees to have a casual conversation over coffee or lunch, anywhere two people can have a reasonably private conversation for at least twenty minutes. This conversation should take place at least once every quarter, although once a month is even better. In the majority of cases, these two simple questions are all you need to ask:

- "Could you tell me about a time in the past month or two when you felt demotivated (or frustrated, or emotionally burnt out)?"

- "Could you tell me about a time in the past month or two when you felt motivated (or excited, or jazzed up)?"

Use language that feels natural for you, and bear in mind that you're not asking these questions simply for the sake of asking questions (like a "fake Diplomat"); you actually want to know the answers. You'll typically find that the issues raised by these questions are as different as people's hair color or their choice of ties. Each person is a little bit different, so find out exactly what motivates and demotivates each individual.

It's natural to wonder if asking these questions will make employees think twice about the demotivators that they face. Could you be putting negative ideas into their heads? My response is that, just because you have an EKG at a checkup, it doesn't mean that you're more likely to have a heart attack. If you are screened for breast or prostate cancer, it doesn't mean that you're more likely to develop those cancers. If you're at risk of a heart attack, getting a good cardiac workup will uncover that hidden risk. It may be scary to learn that your risk is high, and that is why so many don't get the necessary tests—but the tests don't cause the illness. The real question is, do you want to bury your head in the sand, or do you want a team of followers who are happy at work?

Diplomat Technique #2: Ask for Shoves and Tugs, Even If You Know the News Is Bad

Following the attacks of September 11th, 2001, American Express, like many companies, had to undertake painful cuts in order to stay in business. When Ken Chenault, the company CEO at the time, was interviewed, he said the following:

Within 60 days of 9/11 I decided that we had to substantially change our cost structure, which meant that we were going to have to lay off employees. And many people in my top executive team said this is not the time to do it. And from an emotional standpoint, they were absolutely right. The concern that I had was that the future of the company was at stake. And I said we have to do this in a compassionate way with our employees. But we have to do it.[20]

It was a difficult time, and it's truly unfortunate that layoffs were required, but Chenault didn't do what many CEOs would have done—make the cuts and then hide in his office to avoid the emotional hurt. Unlike "fake Diplomats," Chenault made the cuts with as much sensitivity as possible and then he surveyed his employees. As he puts it, and the emphasis in bold is mine, "People said, Ken, if you're going to lay off basically 12% of the workforce, the last thing you want to do is to do a survey on it. **And I said not only are we going to survey the employees but we're going to survey the people that we laid off. Because from a leadership standpoint everyone has to be held accountable.**"[21]

One telltale sign of a true Diplomat is that they will ask for, listen to, and act on their people's motivators and demotivators (i.e., Shoves and Tugs), even if they anticipate bad news.

Diplomat Technique #3: Connect Personally

A newly hired manager recently sent me this letter detailing how he connected with his new employees, even though they were bitter and cynical, due to their previous leaders, who were extremely poor managers. I'm sharing it here because it demonstrates how incorporating the Diplomat style doesn't have to be difficult, if you're willing to exert just a little bit of personal energy, attention and time.

Dear Mark,
I wanted to share this technique because I think it could really benefit your readers. I just joined this company a year ago and I was hired to oversee a large team. This

team previously had three managers in two years, the lowest employee engagement scores in the company and obscenely high employee turnover. In all of my previous leadership roles, retention has always been a priority and top of mind. One of my strategies is to connect individually with as many team members as possible and attempt to create a professional/personal relationship. But honestly, it was hard with this team because they were so bitter and cynical after all of their bad experiences with the previous terrible leaders.

During my first two months on the job, I noticed a large number of my technical team sporting Pink Floyd T-shirts from time to time. As I'm always looking to engage them on something other than a professional level, I began searching for a hook that I could use to initiate a conversation. That hook came when I learned of a Pink Floyd Tribute band that had scheduled a performance in town. I looked up some information about the band and asked those I had observed wearing the shirts if they were familiar with the band. The conversation led to a general discussion of the music they were interested in. That initial discussion has since evolved into other areas, family, work, their concerns, suggestions, feedback and even compliments. This technique could include anything that is of interest to employees. Once you figure out their interests, educate yourself a bit on the subject and look for a hook to initiate a conversation. The key, I believe, is to avoid the obvious, like talking about major or local sporting events or the weather, and really scout for their niche interests. That's where you will get the best bang for the buck.

In my experience you need to move the relationship from one that is strictly professional to one that is professional/personal. The kind where your team sees you as someone who cares about more than just their production. The differentiation is that you, as an employer, are a "kindred spirit" with similar interests. With that belief, people are much less likely to accept another position unless it's truly a much better opportunity. And I know this works because our employee turnover has dropped by a huge 83% in my first twelve months on the job. We just completed our first employee engagement survey since I took over and our overall scores are up by more than 40%. We've still got a lot of work to do, but my boss tells me that he's never seen my department this engaged.

Thank you, Mark, for letting me share.

Bill

First, I'm very grateful to Bill for sharing his story. And second, what's clear from his letter is that it didn't take much at all for Bill to break through the bitterness and cynicism felt by these employees. It required only genuine interest, caring and a willingness to engage with people directly. And, of course, a little extra time.

Bill never would have gained the Pink Floyd insight if he had not been out of his office, interacting with his people. And while bonding over Pink Floyd, or music in general, might not work for everyone, there are thousands of potential connections that a leader could make with their employees. And those connections, in turn, are the key to deepening your relationships with your employees.

WHAT TYPES OF EMPLOYEES DO AND DON'T WORK WELL WITH THE DIPLOMAT

My research has revealed several characteristics that positively correlate with idealizing the Diplomat leadership style. I discovered these characteristics by assessing and analyzing the personality characteristics of employees and then measuring how they respond to the Diplomat leadership style. Here's what I found:

People who idealize the Diplomat leadership style are more likely to enjoy being part of a group and working with others. This is not at all surprising, especially given that one of the Diplomat's leadership characteristics is a desire for an environment in which employees genuinely like one another. Of course, not everyone prioritizes liking their coworkers; people who idealize the Pragmatist style, for example, are more likely to thrive in a competitive environment. But the employees who idealize the Diplomat are significantly more likely to appreciate being and working with their coworkers.

Similarly, the person who idealizes the Diplomat style is more likely to forgive people who have hurt them and is less likely to hold grudges. Compared with the folks who idealize the Pragmatist style, who admit that they are more likely to hold grudges, the Diplomat's followers are more tolerant and forgiving. Note that this isn't a value judgement; it's just an observation based on the data.

Given the collegial environments created by Diplomats, it's not surprising that the followers who like this style try to be polite to other people all of the time, and they try not to upset or irritate others. There are certainly workplaces that could be described as "rough-and-tumble," but those cultures are generally not led by Diplomats. Not only does the Diplomat desire a friendly, harmonious workplace, but the Diplomat's followers are more likely than most to enjoy chitchat and social conversations with others, and to be very accepting of people with different views and opinions.

When it comes to making decisions, the followers who idealize the Diplomat style are more likely to trust their gut and intuition. By contrast, those who idealize the Pragmatist leadership style are more likely to use careful, detailed analysis to make decisions. One style isn't better than another, but in the Diplomat's environment, gut feelings tend to hold more sway. This, in part, is because the followers who thrive here are also more likely to openly express their emotions and feelings.

CHAPTER 3

THE STEWARD

In January of 2018, Eric Schmidt stepped down as Executive Chairman of Alphabet, Google's parent company. Recruited in 2001 by Google co-founders Larry Page and Sergey Brin, Eric served as CEO until 2011 before becoming Executive Chairman. When Eric started at Google, the company had $90 million in annual revenue; today it's projected to be around $100 billion.

What was it that compelled Google's founders to take a pass on every other person interested in the job, many with stellar qualifications, and target Eric as their choice for CEO? In addition to Eric's obvious business acumen, Larry, Sergey and even Eric, jokingly referred to him as the "adult supervision." And in many ways, it's a good description of many Steward leaders.

When Eric was recently interviewed by LinkedIn founder Reid Hoffman, he was asked to recount his experience when he joined Google. His answer, below, is a classic Steward response:

These two young men [Google founders Larry Page and Sergey Brin] are brilliant, crazy, and unreliable, and we need a CEO that can manage them. ... I had a list of things they needed to do, and we went and did them. Almost all small companies are full of energy and no process. My list was straightforward: internationalization plans, sales plans, product plans, accounting, etc. My first meeting at Google was like being at a graduate school full of interesting people with no deadlines or deliverables.

In the same interview, Reid asked Eric, "What was the role of the CEO?" and Eric again gave a very Steward-like answer: "My role was to manage the chaos. You need to have someone to run fast and have a good product sense. That was Larry and Sergey. My job was to organize the world around them."[1]

THE STEWARD STYLE DEFINED

Stewards rate high in Structure and Directiveness and low in Challenge and Feeling. Overall, when we chart Stewards' scores on these four factors, they look something like the following (the bars represent the range of scores for each of the factors with the lines inside the bars representing where the majority of scores fall):

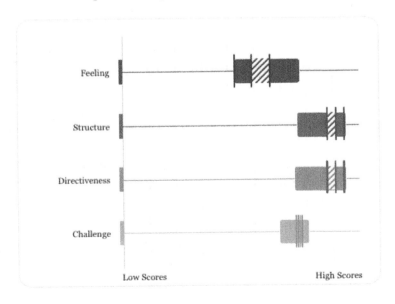

Rating high in Structure and Directiveness means that the Steward leads with significant emphasis placed upon formal procedures, rules, and policies. Much like the "adult supervision" role assumed by Eric Schmidt at Google, the Steward also stresses stability and predictability, typically retains the final decision-making authority, tells employees exactly how tasks and projects should be performed and works harder and longer than anyone else on the team. If you work for a Steward, then there's no mystery around what happens if you fail to do your work satisfactorily; the Steward makes consequences abundantly clear, before poor work has a chance to occur.

Tim Cook, CEO of Apple, is another example of a leader who exemplifies a number of Steward characteristics. Walter Isaacson in his book, *Steve Jobs,* recounts this example of Cook as a leader:

> At a meeting early in his tenure, Cook was told of a problem with one of Apple's Chinese suppliers. "This is really bad," he said. "Someone should be in China driving this." Thirty minutes later, he looked at an operations executive sitting at the table and unemotionally asked, "Why are you still here?" The executive stood up, drove directly to the San Francisco airport, and bought a ticket to China. He became one of Cook's top deputies.[2]

"Why are you still here?" It's a simple, pointed question, and with just those five words Cook clearly communicated exactly how he would like this task to be performed. It's also clear from this example that there was no wiggle room here. Leaving the office in the middle of the day to catch an unexpected 13-hour flight to China to fix a problem is a pretty big request. The executive who followed Cook's directive clearly knew the consequences of not performing as expected, and so, as extraordinary as the request may have seemed, he obliged without question.

If this example makes you wonder what it's like to follow a leader like Tim Cook, consider this comment I found on the question-and-answer site Quora. It comes from an Apple employee responding to the query: "What it's like to work for Tim Cook?" "No one knows the detail of their business better than Tim." This employee also noted, "There is no time for small talk, only purposeful communication in small bite-sized pieces," and "Building your career through job changes makes you a job hopper (read: untrustworthy). Endurance rules."[3]

"Why are you still here?" is certainly a strong indicator that Cook is a fan of using "purposeful communication in small, bite-sized pieces." "Endurance rules" when working for the Steward, but this is not a leader who prioritizes pushing employees to develop their weaknesses or to give maximal, 100% effort. Nor does the Steward expend a lot of energy asking employees about their motivators and demotivators. Exploring the personal needs of employees and building an environment in which employees genuinely like one another is low on the Steward's radar. Instead, the Steward values rules, process and cooperation.

Just as that Apple employee said about Cook, the Steward knows the detail of their business better than anyone. These leaders are the rock of their organization; dependable, loyal and helpful, and they provide a stabilizing and calming force for their employees. They believe that a chain is only as strong as its weakest link, and they move only as fast as the whole chain will allow, taking care and time to help those who struggle to keep up. Working for the Steward offers employees the opportunity to be part of a well-oiled machine. Followers of the Steward will find security, consistency and cohesion at work.

Another example of a leader who embodies many of the Steward characteristic is Chuck Robbins, CEO of Cisco Systems, the American manufacturer of networking hardware. When former Cisco CEO John Chambers stepped down, turning the reins over to Chuck, he compared their leadership styles by saying, "I tend to be more command and control, telling people to make it so. [Chuck] makes the process part of his decision…. Chuck is just an execution machine, he takes vision and strategy and turns them into results."[4]

Nike CEO Mark Parker also embodies many of the characteristics of the Steward leadership style. Consider, for example, this account of Parker's leadership style:

> When Parker noted that Nike's R&D department was exploring a total of 350 new ideas, he recognized that this number was too high. He told the group that they had too many projects. He pushed the staff to make some hard choices. Then he got personally involved, not in personally editing out projects but working with his department to set up criteria to evaluate what things the company needs to accomplish. With Parker's involvement, the R&D team cut the idea list down to 50.[5]

Working for the Steward may not offer great opportunities for individual glory or an adrenaline rush, nor provide lots of personal warmth, but it does provide great opportunities for team success.

Stewards are often found in mission-critical areas of the organization and they are often relied upon by leaders in other divisions. For the appropriate people, working for the Steward is a great situation.

STRENGTHS AND WHERE THE STEWARD STYLE WORKS BEST

All leadership styles work better in some contexts than in others. For example, the process-driven Steward might not be the ideal style to lead a company that sells pedestrian products and no innovation. They also may lack what is needed to provide a sufficiently audacious goal or wild, crazy idea to kick this type of company out of its doldrums. However, there are many contexts in which the Steward shines, including when:

- Employees aren't clear about what's expected of them.
- Employees argue over their performance reviews.
- You're spending too much time dealing with tricky personalities.
- People have great ideas, but poor execution.
- People waste time on the wrong activities.

Let's look at each of these situations in more detail.

Employees Aren't Clear about What's Expected of Them

Remember the Tim Cook example above where an Apple operations executive hopped a flight to China to fix a supplier problem? When Tim was initially informed of the supplier problem, his first response was "Someone should be in China driving this." As we can intuit from the outcome, Tim clearly expected a particular operations executive to respond by immediately getting up from the table and catching a plane to China. And yet, thirty minutes later Tim had to look directly at that executive and ask, "Why are you still here?" Shouldn't this executive have known that when Tim says, "Someone should be in China driving this," he means that someone should get up from the table and start his trip to "be in China?"

Examples of employees who are unclear about what is expected of them abound in companies around the world. Leaders assume that everyone knows what they mean when they issue a directive, and yet, thirty minutes or thirty days later, they're staring at a follower asking, "Why are you still here?"

One of my recent studies asked more than 30,000 employees to rate the statement, "I know whether my performance is where it should be." Ideally, every employee on earth would say "Absolutely, I always know whether my performance is where it should be." Sadly, my study found that only 29% of respondents said they "Always" know whether their performance is where it should be and 14% said they "Frequently" know. By contrast, 36% responded that they "Never" or "Rarely" know, and 21% said they only "Occasionally" know.

When I report these statistics to leaders, it blows their minds. Everyone who has ever held a leadership position has at least several, if not hundreds or even thousands of examples of a time when they gave a directive, and, to their surprise, it wasn't executed or was executed incorrectly. In part, the reason why this happens comes from a natural human tendency to assume that, "People think just like me." Have you ever been at a party, engaged in neutral small talk, and someone breaks in with a strong, one-sided comment about a political issue, assuming that you share their side? It's a pretty common phenomenon; first, we trust that our beliefs are correct, and second, we assume that anyone who is reasonably bright must believe as we do.

When we bring this cognitive schema into the workplace, and, for example, I say to a room of twenty people, "Someone should be in China driving this," I fully expect that Bob over there will hear me and understand that, "OK, wow, the boss just said that I had better get out of this chair and go to China immediately." I may trust that others comprehend the meaning of my words, but real-life experience repeatedly demonstrates that assuming people think "just like me" often fails and can even prove dangerously wrong.

Another reason why only 29% of employees "Always" know that their performance is where it should be, is that many people practice "leadership by aphorism." Leaders are great at generating slogans to ostensibly motivate and direct people's behavior. I'm pretty sure you've heard at least a few of these...

- Work smarter, not harder.
- Leadership's not a title, it's a behavior.
- Listen in such a way that others love to speak to you.
- Treat customers as your top priority.
- Lead by example.
- Take ownership of problems and be accountable.

I've seen every one of those slogans plastered on banners and posters that hang in offices around the world. These are all lovely sentiments, but are any of them really sufficient to direct employees to deliver the performance behaviors you desire? Take the phrase, "Treat customers as a priority." If I'm an employee hearing this, am I to interpret that I should give our products or services away for free? Is that treating customers as a priority? Maybe I should cancel my staff meeting if a customer calls during that time with a simple question. Is that treating customers as a priority? How do I handle customers who aren't profitable? What about customers who blame us for their own mistakes? The aphorism "Treat customers as a priority" only sounds like good behavioral instruction when you don't probe it too intensely.

Now let's contrast "leadership by aphorism" with some of the Steward's characteristics; Stewards clearly communicate to employees exactly how tasks and projects should be performed, as well as the consequences of unsatisfactory work.

When I had the opportunity to work with Terry Byrnes, Vice President of Customer Satisfaction at Harrah's Entertainment, we directed his team to define "Treat customers as a priority" in Steward-like detail. For example, they identified a series of "Never Acceptable" behaviors that clearly directed employees not to:

- Guess or provide information of doubtful accuracy to guests.
- Send a guest away without a suitable answer or assurance to follow up.

- Fail to report new or difficult guest questions or situations to a supervisor for investigation.
- Start a shift unprepared to answer the most common and important guest questions, such as the hours, prices, times and locations of key property features and events.
- Complain or speak negatively to guests about co-workers, management and the company.

These are all very specific performance behavior descriptions. A Harrah's employee, armed with this list, will know exactly what not to do. And, they would have a tough time saying, "But I didn't know," after receiving the performance feedback from a manager that they failed to satisfy a guest's question or spoke negatively to a guest.

The Harrah's team also identified key customer service "Role Model" guidelines:

- When you don't know the answer to a guest question, thank your guest for their patience and maintain ownership until you find someone to help.
- Report new or difficult guest questions to your supervisor so they can investigate and get back to you.
- Make it easy for your guests to get answers to their questions by knowing the hours, prices, times and locations of key property features and events, or by directing them to a user-friendly resource with this information.
- Be optimistic and communicate positively to guests about co-workers, management and the company.

A stranger who has never been to a Harrah's property could walk in off the street, read these lists of behaviors, and tell you exactly what it means to treat customers as a priority. These behavioral guidelines are clear, concise and there's no room for

misinterpretation. It is, of course, the responsibility of the company to support customer service, not a stranger's, but behavioral guidelines must be this specific to be effective.

If you have already, in Steward-like fashion, told your employees exactly how tasks and projects should be performed, and made clear the consequences of unsatisfactory work, then perhaps you don't need to channel your inner Steward. But if your workplace is like most, where only 29% of employees "Always" know if their performance is where it should be, then this is a great opportunity to set expectations with Steward-like clarity.

Employees Argue Over Their Performance Reviews

See if this situation sounds familiar: Pat manages a team of engineers at a large tech company. It's annual performance review time, and Chris is first on her list. Chris' performance is good but not great. His technical skills are very good, but he is not particularly collaborative, nor does he contribute in team meetings. Pat calls Chris into her office and says, "Chris, I'm giving you a 'Meets Expectations' in this year's review. Your technical skills are excellent, but your teamwork could use some improvement."

Chris looks at Pat in disbelief; "What are you talking about— 'Meets Expectations?' I'm one of the best engineers on the team!"

"That's not how I see it, Chris," says Pat. "I think your teamwork could use some improvement. Specifically, I'd like to see you be more collaborative and to contribute in our development meetings."

"What does that even mean?" asks Chris.

"You know, help out your colleagues, speak more. It's not a complicated concept," replies Pat.

To which Chris sarcastically retorts, "So I should do their jobs for them? Maybe stop doing my assignments and follow them around every day?"

Pat, now at the brink of losing her cool, says, "Chris, I find it difficult to believe that you can't understand concepts this simple. I think you know exactly what I'm saying."

Boss/employee conversations like the one Pat and Chris just had occur in practically every company on Earth. The topic isn't always teamwork, but it will be about a performance aspect in which a leader wants an employee to improve. And just like Pat and Chris, the discussion turns into a non-productive debate with both parties arguing the "true" meaning of teamwork, customer service, accuracy, communication, responsiveness, attention to detail, and more.

It's no wonder that managers and employees have disagreements about whether their performance "meets" or "exceeds" expectations. Remember that only 29% of employees say they "Always" know if their performance is where it should be. When you experience these types of disagreements, it's typically a sign that your team or company could use more of the Steward leadership style. Many organizations believe that there is already enough "process" in place for communicating performance expectations to employees. But unless you have been leveraging the Steward leadership style, it's quite likely that your current process is either poorly executed or poorly designed.

Don't make the mistake of believing that because you've mandated annual performance reviews, that your organization already has enough "process." Try this interesting exercise: Ask your employees how often they would like to receive feedback from you about their performance. Is it yearly, quarterly, monthly, weekly or even daily? I can virtually guarantee that not one of your good employees, those who want to minimize mistakes and to grow and develop, will respond that they would like yearly feedback; it's much too infrequent. For the same reason, hardly anyone will respond that quarterly feedback is adequate. Most good employees will choose monthly or weekly feedback, with some high-achiever types opting for daily feedback.

Note that I said that no "good" employees will choose yearly feedback. There may be one or two who respond "yearly," just as a few may respond that they "never" want feedback. It should be obvious why these folks are not going to be your best people.

Once you discover how frequently your good employees want feedback, go ahead and provide that feedback. Make it part of your process. One of the better practices that high-performing Stewards often adopt is monthly coaching sessions with their employees. It's easy to do. Each month, have a sit-down, at which you discuss the employee's high and low points, learning opportunities, and areas where they could elevate their performance. This conversation doesn't obviate the need for a leader to provide continual, real-time performance feedback, but it does offer a guarantee that employees won't have to wait all year to learn whether their performance is where it should be.

You're Spending Too Much Time
Dealing with Tricky Personalities

You may remember the financial crisis of 2007-2008. One of the more well-known players in that drama was Citigroup, often called the first great financial supermarket. Citigroup's CEO at the time, Sandy Weill, was even named by Time Magazine as one of the 25 People to Blame for the Financial Crisis.[6]

One of the issues surrounding Citigroup was their size, the epitome of the phrase, "too big to fail." But, they also may have been too big to manage, especially for Sandy Weill. A decade before the crisis, when Citicorp and Travelers Group merged to form Citigroup, there was a choice of CEOs: John Reed, who was CEO of Citicorp, and Sandy Weill, CEO of Travelers Group. This is how Reed describes it (the emphasis in bold is mine):

"After a lot of yack-yack, the board chose to leave Sandy in. I argued against that—not because I disliked Sandy, but because I didn't think he was the right guy to run the combined entity. He did not, from my point of view, have the skills to run the big company that we had produced. He wasn't a process manager. He ran the place by people and personalities. The company was too big for that."[7]

Running a company "by people and personalities" is often a telltale sign that your organization needs a bit more of the Steward leadership style. Typically, a phrase like "people and personalities" means that a company and its leaders are spending a great deal of time attempting to discern people's motives, needs, wants, political aims, machinations, etc. Or, they're dealing with brilliant, but difficult, employees. While there are occasions where anticipating machinations is useful, it's problematic when leaders regularly spend their scarce resources on corporate politics, rather than answering simple questions, such as, "Is this team producing results?" or "How do we make more money?" or "How do I get employees to meet expectations?"

To be clear, I'm not saying that a dispassionate Steward approach is a universally ideal leadership style. But when your days are spent on corporate politics, or dealing with Talented Terrors and Bless Their Hearts, then a less personal, and more dispassionately factual approach, is likely in order.

Talented Terrors and Bless Their Hearts are two types of low performers that often consume leaders' time, especially when leaders fail to tell employees exactly how tasks and projects should be performed, and about the consequences of unsatisfactory work. If either of the following two descriptions sound similar to any members of your team, then you should probably consider employing some degree of Steward leadership style.

Let's start by thinking about performance as having two dimensions: skills and attitude. You can undoubtedly come up with others, but my numerous studies show that almost all attributes of performance are ultimately encompassed by skills or attitude.

We call the people with great attitudes, but lousy skills, the "Bless Their Hearts." To translate for anyone who hasn't spent much time in the American Deep South, "bless your heart" is a Southern phrase that basically means: "Thanks for trying, but what you just did was totally clueless. And you're lucky my code of Southern gentility prohibits me from saying anything more, because I might just slip and say something really mean." [Note: While I currently live in the South, I grew up in the North, where we instead use the phrase, "God love 'em," when what we really mean is: "I'm sure they meant well, but boy that was dumb."]

Regardless of the phrase you use, if it describes someone in your organization, then it's time to rethink that person's performance potential. Someone with a great attitude, who is really trying and genuinely wants to please, but who repeatedly fails to get the job done right and just can't hack the skills, isn't an "almost" high performer. God love 'em, but that person is a low performer, and no amount of amazing attitude is going to make up for it. No low performer should be admitted to the elite club that is your organization. You can root for that person every step of the way (and who doesn't want to see a plucky underdog succeed?), but it doesn't change the employee's sub-par performance.

The other category of low performer sits diametrically opposite the Bless Their Hearts. These people have great skills but lousy attitudes, earning them the title "Talented Terrors." These low performers are "emotional vampires." They won't actually suck your blood, but the frustration of dealing with them will suck the life out of you.

Talented Terrors are by far the most difficult category of low performer to manage. They're highly skilled, and they can prove it. This lulls leaders into complacency during performance reviews, because "nobody this skilled could possibly get a low score, right?" Think about the Talented Terrors you employ. No matter how badly they act on a given day, when the Chairman of the Board walks by their desk, it's all good humor and positivity. "Hello Sir, wonderful day we're having! You're looking more fit than ever. Have you lost weight? I just finished reading your letter to the shareholders, and it was brilliant as always, Sir!" Of course, as soon as the Chairman leaves, the sunshine turns to dark and threatening clouds and the Talented Terror returns to sucking the life out of you and everyone else around them with their bad attitude.

Owing to the Steward's dedication to clear expectations, formal procedures, rules, policies, stability and predictability, these leaders are far less likely to get caught up in the drama brought on by Talented Terrors. The Steward is unlikely to worry about the Talented Terror's "potential" or why their attitude is so poor; the employee will simply be evaluated against whatever criteria the Steward has clearly defined.

People Have Great Ideas, but Poor Execution

It's not uncommon to see teams plagued by great ideas but lousy execution. For the past few decades, companies have sometimes fetishized the breakthrough idea that will completely upend an entire industry; they want to invent the next iPod, iPad or iPhone. But what often gets missed, is that those "iDevices" weren't just great ideas; they were executed to near perfection.

Perhaps you've been in meetings with big-idea, no-execution colleagues. These are the people who might blurt out, mid meeting, "This is a stupid idea. I've got something better we can try instead." They love going against convention, and maybe they can deliver the great idea that unsticks the team's thinking. But when the team has been developing that other idea for six weeks or even six months, and it has been tested and refined, with detailed execution plans, then this type of outburst can be awfully frustrating. Not only can it ruin the dynamics on your team, but it can derail the group from addressing tough execution issues, focusing them instead on the big, sexy breakthrough idea.

One test that can confirm that your group could use more Steward-style leadership, is to assess how often the people on your team leave meetings with concrete tasks, complete with deadlines. And then, track how often those tasks are actually accomplished.

Years ago, I conducted a study called "Why CEOs Get Fired." It's a commonly-held belief that CEOs get fired, or are forced to resign or retire under pressure, because of "current financial performance." But, that's wrong. During this four-year study, I interviewed 1,087 board members from 286 public, private, business and healthcare organizations that fired, or otherwise forced out, their chief executive. I found that 31% of CEOs are fired for mismanaging change, 28% for ignoring customers, 27% for tolerating low performers, 23% for denying reality and 22% for too much talk and not enough action.

It's the "too much talk, not enough action" factor that I would like to address. While conducting the survey, I heard many comments about CEOs talking the talk, but being unable to walk the walk. Numerous board members complained that CEOs could expound endlessly about grand visions and new strategies, but they would neglect creating a tactical plan for the "who, what, when and where," and/or were unable to provide evidence of any implementation. One board member commented that their former CEO "gives good meetings, but little else."

Big ideas are great, but big ideas without clear execution are a problem for companies and for leaders' careers. If you find that the above rings true with your group, then take a hard look at implementing a bit more of the Steward leadership style.

People Waste Time on the Wrong Activities

I recently conducted a study of several thousand leaders in which I asked them to track their biggest time wasters. Here are the top five that they reported:

1. Meetings that are wasteful because they didn't have a clear point.
2. Meetings that are wasteful because they got far off track.
3. Dealing with low performers that have bad attitudes (Talented Terrors).
4. Dealing with low performers that have poor skills (Bless Their Hearts).
5. Having to nag employees for incomplete work.

I've addressed a number of these time wasters already, but No. 5 is one I have not yet tackled. Having to nag employees to finish their work, or even provide a status update, generally happens when leaders fail to clearly articulate expectations. Often these leaders have become too accommodating of people's excuses, failing to hold employees accountable for not finishing their work or providing status updates.

Regardless of the exact cause, it's a bad sign when people are missing deadlines, or you're forced to chase them down just to get a simple status report. When any of these time wasters start eating away at your day, it's often a signal to employ the Steward's clear expectations, formal procedures, rules, policies, stability and predictability.

WARNING SIGNS THAT THE STEWARD STYLE ISN'T WORKING

Employing a Steward leadership style can deliver great results, but there are times where a leader can venture too far into the Steward realm. The following three signs are warnings that your Steward style is coming across as too stifling and controlling:

Steward Warning Sign #1: You're doing too much managing and not enough coaching

We've all experienced the situation where an employee comes to us with one or more problems that they would like us to solve.

Maybe an employee walks into our office and says, "Hey Boss, I need your help. The other division won't respond to my emails about giving me the data I need to finish my report." And then, that person just waits for us to solve the problem.

Why do employees bring us their problems instead of fixing problems themselves? Occasionally it's because they've tried everything they can think of and they're truly out of ideas. If that's the case, then it's completely legitimate to come to the boss for help. Sadly, much of the time, it's because we've inadvertently trained our employees that we solve their problems for them, and it's because we've solved their problems so many times before.

The irony here is that I regularly hear leaders complain that their employees are "too passive," "too reactive," "they need to think for themselves," or "they don't take enough initiative." Whenever an employee brings you a problem, especially one that you think you know how to solve, you have a decision to make. Should you jump in and solve it yourself (i.e., managing) or should you help the employee discover a solution that may be different than yours (i.e., coaching)?

Many leaders choose the managing option, both because leaders often have a ready solution, and most leaders are type-A personalities that like to jump in and fix things. Choosing to manage is a big temptation for Stewards who have very clear expectations about how things should be done. If those expectations aren't met, then it's a major irritant for Stewards, so it's understandable why they tend to jump right in and start problem solving, manager style. But when leaders choose the managing approach, they deprive their employees of the opportunity to grow, ironically guaranteeing that employees will keep pestering them for solutions. In choosing to manage instead of coach, leaders also deprive themselves of the opportunity to see if their employees can actually generate a solution that's even better than their solution.

Let's go back to the scenario in which an employee comes into your office and says, "Hey Boss, I need your help. The other division won't respond to my emails about giving me the data I need to finish my report." Here are two possible responses to this situation:

- The manager might say, "Darn it, well, let me call them directly and get them straightened out." In the mind of an irritated Steward, this is a simple fix that will result in expectations being met.
- By contrast, a leader who takes more of a coaching approach might say, "OK, well, tell me about the steps you've taken so far. What are you thinking about doing next? How is it the same or different from what you've tried before? If Plan A doesn't work, what might be a good Plan B?

Notice how the coaching approach utilizes lots of questions? That's because the coach, like a great psychologist, is helping the employee analyze the situation and develop multiple strategies.

This coaching approach has three benefits. First, the employee is developing and honing critical thinking skills, tools that can be used for the life of a career. Second, the boss isn't getting sucked into every little employee problem, what we often call "reverse delegation." A coaching approach provides the Steward with time to develop new and better processes, rather than having their days consumed by dealing with every single employee issue. And third, the employee is learning how to take initiative and be proactive.

I'm not advising that a leader can never jump in and solve problems. I am, however, saying that there's a lot to be gained by coaching versus managing. The next time an employee brings you a problem, and before you immediately jump right in to solve it, ask some of the questions I listed above. It's ultimately less work for the leader, and your employees may surprise you with some great and original ideas.

Steward Warning Sign #2: You're micromanaging
Imagine that you're sitting at your desk, intensely focused on writing a big report, when you start to feel a weird tingling on the back of your neck. You try to refocus, furrowing your brow and redoubling your efforts, but you can't shake the disquieting sense that you're being watched. Finally, you give up and slowly turn around in your chair. "Ahhrh! Jeezum! What the?!?!?!?" you shriek as you flail out of your seat. Looming a few inches behind you, watching your every move, is your boss.

Not every micromanaging boss lurks in the office waiting to startle you with their best Norman Bates impression. But whether it's a boss who skulks about, emails employees incessantly for status updates, or engages in other micromanaging behavior, being on the receiving end of micromanaging is frustrating and even demoralizing.

Are you guilty of micromanaging? Here are two questions to help you understand the situation more objectively: First, do you ever feel frustrated when you receive a finished product from an employee because the work was done differently than you would have done it? Second, do you ever feel a twinge of satisfaction when you find mistakes, even small ones, in your employees' work? If you answered "yes" to either of those questions, then you might have taken the Steward leadership style a bit too far.

Why do bosses micromanage? Are they sadistically trying to cause their employees pain? The honest answer is that there are some malformed personalities scattered throughout the world's managerial ranks. However, most of the time when a boss is micromanaging, the root cause isn't sadism, it's fear. There are many reasons why bosses experience fear. Some bosses fear a loss of control. For instance, if you're an individual contributor programmer, you can resolve a lot of issues by yourself. You type your lines of code and if something goes wrong, you fix it. But if you're a manager and something goes wrong, you can't just hop in front of your computer and fix it. As manager, you oversee a bunch of programmers and your job is to convince them to go fix the problem. It's one of the great ironies of having managerial authority; your title gets bigger, but your personal control gets smaller, and the bigger your title, the less personal control you have.

Other leaders experience the fear that comes from having a healthy ego. Bosses often start their careers as high-performing individual contributors. They're expert in their individual roles, they get noticed for doing superior work and then are promoted into a supervisory job. They were the best person in their individual role, but now they're managing a group of people who aren't as good as they are. The fear here is that if they put their name on work that's not as good as they could have done themselves, then they will look bad.

Steward Warning Sign #3: You're not open to hearing suggestions for improvement

Sometimes a leader can get so focused on giving directions, setting clear expectations about how they would like work performed, and on establishing effective rules and procedures, that they won't listen when one of their employees comes to them with good ideas for improvement.

In 2017, I surveyed more than 27,000 leaders and employees, and discovered that only 24% say that their leader "Always" encourages and recognizes suggestions for improvement, while 16% say their leader "Never" does so. Even if we combine those who say their leader "Always" (24%) or "Frequently" (23%) encourages and recognizes suggestions for improvement (that would be 47%), that still leaves more than half of employees (53%) feeling that their leader is not doing a good job encouraging and recognizing suggestions for improvement.

This is problematic on several fronts. First, it's entirely possible that the employees on the frontlines have ideas that are substantially better than what the leader is currently demanding. Perhaps the leader has set clear expectations that a project is to be completed within three days, but an employee offers a simple process tweak that would reduce time to completion to two days. Every leader would welcome a 33% reduction in the time required to complete the project, would they not? Well, the smart ones would, but some leaders become so entrenched in the idea that "my way is the best way," that they don't know how to loosen the reins and allow the employee to improve the process.

Failing to encourage suggestions for improvement also damages a leader's ability to keep people engaged at work. When we asked employees if they would recommend their company as a great organization to work for, we found that 62% of employees who say their leader "Always" encourages and recognizes suggestions for improvement, also strongly recommend their company as a great organization to work for. By contrast, only 5% of employees who say that their leader "Never" encourages and recognizes suggestions for improvement, strongly recommend their company as a great organization to work for.

In essence, if someone thinks that their leader "Always" encourages and recognizes suggestions for improvement, then they're about twelve times more likely to recommend the company as a great employer. If you've ever wondered just how demoralizing it is to work for someone with an overly-controlling leadership style, that particular statistic indicates just how destructive it really is.

SHOULD YOU EVER TRY TO BECOME MORE OF A STEWARD?

Even if Steward isn't your default leadership style, there are times when you might consider employing some of the Steward characteristics described heretofore. Perhaps your employees aren't clear about what's expected of them and you must give the same directives time and time again. Or, maybe you're seeing employees consistently disagree with, and argue about, their performance reviews. It may be that your time is consumed managing personalities rather than tasks and projects, or that your team has brilliant ideas but just don't execute on any of them.

Any of these scenarios could signal a need for some Steward leadership style. So how do you actually adopt a Steward style? Here are two techniques to get you started:

Steward Technique #1: Word Pictures
Think back to my study, in which only 29% of people said that they "Always" know whether their performance is where it should be, 14% "Frequently" know, 36% of people said that they "Never" or "Rarely" know, and 21% said they only "Occasionally" know. To emulate the Steward style, this is the very first issue a leader must correct. And to accomplish that, I recommend a technique I call Word Pictures.

Word Pictures is a training technique whereby you paint a clear behavioral verbal picture that tells employees exactly what behaviors you expect, broken down into three levels: "Needs Work," "Good Work" and "Great Work." Remember how leaders at Harrah's Entertainment wanted all employees to "treat customers as a priority," but they realized that aphorism was just too vague, so they identified the specific customer service behaviors that they wanted to see every employee perform? To do Great Work treating customers as a priority, they required employees to know the hours, prices, times and locations of key property features and events, so they could readily answer guest questions. Other Great Work behaviors required employees to be optimistic and to speak positively to guests about co-workers, management and the company.

Similarly, Harrah's leaders outlined some Needs Work behaviors (i.e., poor or bad work). For instance, poorly performing employees who failed to treat customers as a priority would start their shifts unprepared to answer the most common and important guest questions. Complaining or speaking negatively to guests about co-workers, management and the company was also in the Needs Work behavior category.

The key here is twofold. First, Harrah's leaders didn't use vague platitudes; they identified specific behavioral expectations that they wanted employees to meet. Second, they didn't just tell employees which behaviors were desirable; they also outlined undesirable behaviors.

Recently, a CEO called me to gripe about the lack of accountability among his employees. I didn't fully understand what he meant by the word "accountability;" on its own, it's an awfully vague term. So, I asked him to provide examples of the specific employee behaviors around accountability that he found the most problematic. Here's what he came up with in the Needs Work category:

- When new changes are implemented, I resist the changes and push for a return to the "status quo."
- When breakdowns or missed communications occur, I engage in finger-pointing and blaming others.
- When I make mistakes or miss deadlines, I offer excuses (e.g., "I couldn't get it done, because…").
- When the going gets tough or intense, I become frantic, lose focus, and get emotionally worked up.
- I avoid extra work, and when on a team, I allow my coworkers to do most of the work.

Those are the Needs Work behaviors, the actions that employees absolutely should not do. Next, I asked this CEO to provide specific examples of positive employee behaviors around accountability that he would like his employees to exhibit. Here's what he came up with for Good Work behaviors:

- I openly support change initiatives.
- I don't wait to be told to take action and I find opportunities to help complete projects more quickly and effectively.
- I accept personal responsibility for quality and timeliness of work without making excuses or blaming others.
- I meet my commitments, and if it looks like I won't personally be able to meet a commitment, then I take responsibility for implementing an alternative that ensures that the commitment is still met.

If I'm an employee reading those descriptions of Needs Work and Good Work, then I know what not to do, and I know what I should do to meet my leader's expectations. But, I might wonder, "How do I exceed those expectations?" That is where the Great Work category comes into play. Here's how this CEO defined the behaviors of employees that do Great Work:

I do everything in the Good Work category, plus...

- I encourage and convince my fellow employees to support change initiatives.
- I actively redirect conversations with my colleagues to stop them from making excuses or blaming others.
- If I uncover an unexpected problem, then I immediately remedy the situation. In addition, I bring the problem to the attention of others on my team, so we can develop a root-cause solution to prevent anyone else from experiencing the same issue.

If I'm a leader armed with these definitions of Needs Work, Good Work and Great Work, and I actually share them with my team, or develop them collaboratively with my team, then I should never again have employees who don't know whether their performance is where it should be. And, I should never have employees who argue with me about their performance reviews.

Stewards aren't the only leaders who can create and use Word Pictures. Any leader can create Word Pictures, as long as the behaviors described in the three categories of Needs Work, Good Work and Great Work are observable, gradable, verifiable, and explicit. My team and I have developed Word Pictures for innovation, expertise, customer service, accuracy, flexibility, management, communication, financial awareness and hundreds of other topics. It is highly likely that whatever issues you need to improve upon can also be turned into a Word Picture.

I know that Word Pictures can seem painfully explicit. But, by providing transparency about what does, and does not, meet expectations, it's a tool for teaching every employee exactly what they should, and shouldn't, do. It's the Steward's willingness to clearly define expectations, using a tool like Word Pictures, that helps leaders avoid some of the problems that occur when employees are not clear about what's expected of them, or when employees consistently disagree with, and argue about, their performance reviews.

One final note: Word Pictures make employee self-evaluation much more likely. Word Pictures will help to develop your employees' critical self-awareness, and, because of the behavioral specificity and learning design of Word Pictures, your employees will immediately understand where they are lacking, and where they should focus their personal improvement efforts. This frees you from having to shadow each employee, pointing out "opportunities for improvement," because every person on the team now knows exactly what to do, and what not to do.

Steward Technique #2: Run More Effective Meetings
The Steward leadership style can help you to run more efficient and effective meetings. This might seem like a pedestrian area

on which to focus, but not if you recall my study of why CEOs get fired. Remember the board member who commented that their former CEO "gives good meetings, but little else?" When I ask leaders, "What is the number one thing that wastes your time and hinders your productivity?" the nearly universal answer is, "meetings." Whether they are wasteful meetings that don't resolve anything, meetings where everyone talks just to hear themselves speak, or meetings where decisions are never made, meetings are often hated and typically wasteful.

The good news is that while meetings are generally reviled, the problems that make meetings so unpopular can be fixed. Stewards generally run incredibly effective meetings that start on time, foster accountability, engage everyone in the room, stay on topic, and more. The following are six of the biggest gripes about meetings along with a few of the techniques Stewards use to turn bad meetings into highly effective and productive forums for generating better ideas and making smarter decisions.

Meeting Gripe No. 1: Meetings Last Too Long

At the top of the list of gripes are meetings that seem to drag on forever. One issue is that electronic scheduling tools stubbornly assign 30-or 60-minute slots to meetings. When the calendar specifies that, "We are going to spend 60 minutes in a meeting," the tendency is to stretch the meeting content to fill the allotted time. If you remember what you learned back in high school or college science class, you know that gases, such as air or helium inside a balloon, expand to fill the shape of the containers they're in. Meetings are like gas expanding to fill up a room. If you take 20 minutes of content and you stick it in a 60-minute time block, then the content will expand to fill those 60 minutes.

A Statement of Achievement is a simple time management tool that states, "As a result of this meeting, we will have achieved _____." If you can't fill in the blank, then cancel the meeting. If you can fill in the blank, then your meeting has a clear objective. Let meeting attendees know that when you meet that objective, the meeting is over. A Statement of Achievement removes time as the measure of meeting completion and replaces it with achievement. When organizations implement a Statement of Achievement, meetings are more productive and are shortened, on average, by 17 minutes.

Meeting Gripe No. 2: People Who Come Late to Meetings

Latecomers to meetings are annoying and distracting, especially when everyone in the meeting has to backtrack in order to bring that person up to speed. One reason that people don't respect meeting start times is that they view meetings as free. The direct expense may not show up in a budget, but if you calculate the number of people in attendance, the average hourly wage and the length of the meeting, it's clear just how much a meeting costs.

The solution is to stop indulging latecomers. I've seen meetings where, if there are eight people in attendance, they'll order seven donuts, so the last person to show up doesn't get anything to eat. One Board of Directors I know assigns buying dinner to the last person to show up for monthly board meetings. This group tends to meet at upscale restaurants, making the penalty for being the last one there extra painful. I know of an organization that makes people sing when they arrive late to a meeting. Many leaders lock the door when a meeting is scheduled to start to block out latecomers. Whatever action you take, it must be driven by the idea that meeting time is a valuable organizational resource and wasting it is simply not acceptable.

Meeting Gripe No. 3: Nothing Gets Accomplished in Meetings

In far too many meetings, the first 15, 20 or even 30 minutes are spent in idle chitchat, coffee klatches, housekeeping details or catching up from the last meeting. This goes on until someone looks at their watch and says, "Oh my gosh! We've got only 20 minutes left in this meeting. We better start talking about how to respond to this price war situation!"

The most valuable cognitive time in a meeting is at the start, when people's brains are fresh and focused, so prioritize meetings to address the most important topic right away. Ensure that people to show up prepared to work by distributing an agenda, prior to the meeting, that addresses the following four points: the topic to be discussed, why this topic is on the agenda, what we hope to accomplish by discussing this topic and what people should do to prepare for the meeting.

Meeting Gripe No. 4: I Don't Belong in This Meeting
Most people, and especially the most productive people, don't want to sit in a meeting where they're not going to add value. A clearly written agenda enables you to review the list of potential meeting attendees and ask, "Does this person have some special insight or power or influence that this meeting needs to succeed?" If the answer is "Yes," then determine if making this person sit through the entire meeting is the best way to access their input. Some people may need to attend only part of a meeting, or it might make better sense to access their knowledge and input by scheduling a private meeting. A good rule to follow: Your meeting is too big if it includes more people than you can feed with two regular size pizzas.

Meeting Gripe No. 5: No One Pays Attention in Meetings
Whether it's people glancing at their devices while checking out of the conversation or losing the attention of people brought into the meeting just to listen (see gripe No. 4), scanning a meeting room and seeing people zoned out is pretty darn frustrating. It's easy to keep everyone on their toes by regularly asking questions such as:

- "How would you answer someone who asked about the other ideas that we considered, but didn't choose?"
- "Are there any circumstances under which our current decision won't work?"
- "If you could create a solution from scratch, would this be it?"

Questions like those invite meeting participants to feel like part of the process, even if they aren't in an active role. It also sends the clear message that anyone checking out of the meeting will likely be "caught."

Meeting Gripe No. 6: No Follow-Through After Meetings Are Over

If you find yourself holding a meeting to discuss what didn't get accomplished after the last meeting, then it's a clear sign of an accountability issue. Meeting minutes tend to be ineffective at holding people accountable because while they document who said what to whom, they often fail to include action items, who is responsible for fulfilling those action items, and by when. Combat this lack of accountability by concluding every meeting with a quick "roundtable" response to, "What are you personally going to achieve and by when?" Document the responses on a decision grid and distribute it to all meeting attendees. Collectively building a decision grid creates peer pressure that eliminates the excuse, "That got buried somewhere in the meeting and I didn't know I was responsible for it."

Stewards run such effective meetings, because doing so provides norm-setting and signaling effects. In other words, because meetings are ubiquitous, if you can make them more efficient and effective, it establishes a norm in which everything should operate with similar efficiency and effectiveness. And it signals to all employees that the leader takes these norms very seriously. Whether implicitly or explicitly, Stewards tell employees exactly how they would like tasks and projects to be performed, and clearly communicate to employees the consequences of unsatisfactory work.

WHAT TYPES OF EMPLOYEES DO AND DON'T WORK WELL WITH THE STEWARD?

My research has discovered several characteristics that positively correlate with idealizing the Steward leadership style. I discovered these characteristics by assessing and analyzing the personality characteristics of employees, and then measuring how they respond to the Steward leadership style. Here is what I found:

People who idealize the Steward leadership style are more likely to be highly detail-oriented and believe in "dotting the i's and crossing the t's." This is not at all surprising, especially given that one of the Steward's leadership characteristics is emphasizing formal procedures, rules, and policies. Similarly, the Steward's most enthusiastic followers like having rules and detailed processes. While some people like ambiguous and fluid work environments, it is absolutely not the case for people who thrive working under the Steward's leadership style.

The same goes for having a consistent routine. Certainly, there are people who love the adrenaline rush that comes from frequent and unexpected change, but the people that idealize the Steward leadership style definitely prefer consistency and routine. Remember that the Steward emphasizes stability and predictability, so their preference is consistent with that.

In a related vein, the Steward's followers believe that people should do what they're told and follow the rules. They also believe that, in general, people should be satisfied with the status quo and not ask for more than what they have. This is consistent with the Steward's tendency to communicate to employees the consequences of unsatisfactory work. Pro-Steward followers are also more cautious than followers of other leadership styles. They are more likely to believe in the adage, "If it ain't broke, don't break it." And, they're more likely to adhere to the notion that it's better to be safe than risk being sorry.

Finally, given the Steward's emphasis on formal procedures, rules, and policies, and setting clear expectations, it's no surprise that their followers tend to favor making decisions by way of careful, detailed analysis.

CHAPTER 4
THE IDEALIST

Sheryl Sandberg is famous not only because she's the Chief Operating Officer of Facebook, but also because she wrote the book *Lean In*, a bestselling guide to women's empowerment in the workplace. The following, which is one of the most quoted anecdotes from the book, concerns her epiphany about the internal barriers women face in the workplace. The boldface type is mine, and it's used to show emphasis:

> A few years ago, I hosted a meeting for Treasury Secretary Tim Geithner at Facebook. We invited fifteen executives from across Silicon Valley for breakfast and a discussion about the economy. Secretary Geithner arrived with four members of his staff, two senior and two more junior, and we all gathered in our one nice conference room. After the usual milling around, I encouraged the attendees to help themselves to the buffet and take a seat. Our invited guests, mostly men, grabbed plates and food and sat down at the large conference table. Secretary Geithner's team, all women, took their food last and sat in chairs off to the side of the room. I motioned for the women to come sit at the table, waving them over publicly so they

would feel welcomed. They demurred and remained in their seats.

The four women had every right to be at this meeting, but because of their seating choice, they seemed like spectators rather than participants. I knew I had to say something. So, after the meeting, I pulled them aside to talk. I pointed out that they should have sat at the table even without an invitation, but when publicly welcomed, they most certainly should have joined. At first, they seemed surprised, then they agreed.

It was a watershed moment for me. A moment when I witnessed how an internal barrier can alter women's behavior. A moment when I realized that in addition to facing institutional obstacles, women face a battle from within.[1]

It's the last paragraph that tends to get a lot of attention, but for purposes of discussing the Idealist leadership style, I want to highlight the middle paragraph. When Sheryl says, "After the meeting, I pulled them aside to talk. I pointed out that they should have sat at the table even without an invitation," she's exemplifying a classic Idealist behavior; helping someone grow and develop, even if that person didn't explicitly seek assistance.

Sheryl doesn't tell the women from the Treasury Department to sit at the table with the intention to belittle them or cause regret; she's truly concerned about seeing them advance in their careers. Perhaps, they were a bit taken aback when Sheryl first offered the feedback; maybe they even found the feedback tough. But, there's no question that Sheryl's feedback was offered in a spirit of deep caring about their future success.

THE IDEALIST STYLE DEFINED

Idealists rate high in Feeling and Challenge, and lower in Structure and Directiveness. Overall, when we chart Idealists' scores on these four factors, they look something like the following (the bars represent the range of scores for each of the factors with the lines inside the bars representing where the majority of scores fall):

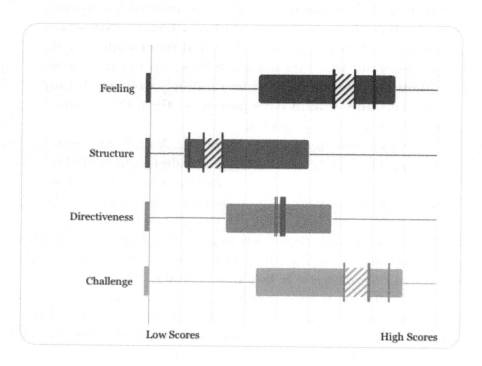

Like the Pragmatist, the Idealist rates high on Challenge, pushing employees to work on strengthening their weaknesses, not just focus only on their strengths, and to give maximal, 100% effort. Unlike the Pragmatist, they balance that Challenge with high levels of Feeling. The Idealist regularly asks employees about their motivators and demotivators, cares deeply about the personal needs of employees, desires an environment in which employees genuinely like one another, and is very concerned that employees find their work personally fulfilling.

David C. Novak, Chairman of Yum! Brands (owner of the brands KFC, Pizza Hut and Taco Bell), emphasized the need for Idealist-level Feeling in this *Corner Office* interview for *The New York Times*:

> What I think a great leader does, a great coach does, is understand what kind of talent you have and then you help people leverage that talent so that they can achieve what they never thought they were capable of. The only way you can do that is to care about the people who work for you. No one's going to care about you unless you care about them. But if you care about someone, genuinely, then they're going to care about you because you're making a commitment and an investment in them.
>
> You show you care by really taking an active interest in the people working for you, and you care enough to give them direct feedback. People are starved for direct feedback. People want to hear how they can do better. Too many leaders don't provide that feedback. So if you take an active interest in someone, you take an active interest in sharing with them your perspective on what they can do to improve.[2]

In many ways the Idealist is like the high school teacher who tells students, "I'm gonna push you hard, but I'm doing this because I care about you and want to see you succeed." We see this reflected in the example above where Sheryl Sandberg pulled aside the women from the Treasury Department and gave them some tough, but necessary, advice about sitting at the table.

Meg Whitman is the former CEO of Hewlett Packard, eBay and more. In 2015, she gave a talk to the students of Stanford's Graduate School of Business and shared the following Idealist career advice that highlights the importance of learning. Once again, the boldface type is mine, used to show emphasis:

So, listen, I think it's a little different graduating from business school today than it was in 1979 when I graduated from business school. That seemed like 100 years ago. First of all, there was not the startup culture that there is today in Silicon Valley and in Austin, Texas and in Boston, Massachusetts. I mean, I don't think anyone really seriously considered starting their own company out of Harvard Business School or joining a startup. It just wasn't what you did. It wasn't really in the menu of things. And I think many of you will join a startup or start a company. **So back then we were thinking "How do we get the very best training for a long career in business? How do we lay the pipe of things that we will need to know through a career?"** And so that's why I was interested in marketing and I decided to go to what I perceived as the very best company in marketing and that was P&G because you have to remember, I had no work experience between undergraduate and graduate school. So, I was all about the training, and I have to say, it's really quite fun because I now sit on the P&G board, so talk about coming full circle. But what I learned at P&G has kept me in good stead until this day. **I was all about going to the best companies to get the best training to prepare for what I believed would be a long career.**[3]

In another speaking engagement, Meg spoke to the students at Duke's business school, where she shared this story about how she applied this philosophy of learning after she was fired from her job as CEO of FTD, the floral and gift company. Again, the boldface is mine for emphasis:

I was at FTD for about a year and a half and got fired. So, think about that for a second. I mean, I remember sort of like "Wow, OK, that's different." And you feel terrible about it for a while; you feel like you let yourself down, and you feel like you let the investors down, and then you just say, **"What am I going to learn from that?"** And you get back in the arena... **I love to learn. I'm constantly trying to figure out "What could we do differently?"** What would make an outcome different this time?[4]

For Meg, Sheryl, David and other Idealists, learning is of paramount importance. Whether one is succeeding or failing, there is always something to be learned.

The Idealist will challenge employees, but they typically won't retain the final decision-making authority, tell employees exactly how they would like tasks and projects to be performed, or clearly communicate to employees the consequences of unsatisfactory work. Nor is it common for the Idealist to emphasize formal procedures, rules, and policies. Idealists are high-energy achievers who believe in the positive potential of everyone around them. They want to learn and grow, and they want everyone else on the team to do the same. They're often charismatic, drawing others to them with their intuition and idealism. They're open-minded and prize creativity from themselves and others.

Working for Idealists offers the chance to be creative and to express oneself. Employees find that they have an equal voice and that they learn by doing. Working for the Idealist often provides a very democratic experience. There isn't as much process and structure as with some other leaders (like Stewards), and that can be a plus or minus depending on the employee. Idealist leaders are often found doing creative work. It's not unusual to find them sitting around a table brainstorming with like-minded individuals.

For the appropriate people, working for the Idealist is a great situation. Not only do Idealists help their followers learn and grow, they generally apply this learning philosophy to themselves as well. For example, when an interviewer asked legendary investor

Warren Buffett, "How do you keep up with all the media and information that goes on in our crazy world and in your world of Berkshire Hathaway? What's your media routine?" he responded: "I read and read and read. I probably read five to six hours a day. I don't read as fast now as when I was younger. But I read five daily newspapers. I read a fair number of magazines. I read 10-Ks. I read annual reports. I read a lot of other things, too. I've always enjoyed reading. I love reading biographies, for example."[5]

When Microsoft founder Bill Gates was asked "What role does reading play in your life?" he responded, "It is one of the chief ways that I learn and has been since I was a kid. These days, I also get to visit interesting places, meet with scientists and watch a lot of lectures online. But reading is still the main way that I both learn new things and test my understanding."[6]

While most successful leaders, regardless of leadership style, encourage constant growth and development in themselves and their followers, the Idealist generally makes this a much higher priority.

STRENGTHS AND WHERE THE IDEALIST STYLE WORKS BEST

All leadership styles work better in some contexts than in others. For example, the learning-oriented Idealist might not be the ideal person to lead a company in a dying industry with fairly mindless jobs and a corporate culture accepting of low levels of employee engagement and high turnover. However, there are lots of contexts in which the Idealist does shine, including when:

- There are lots of younger employees.
- Employees are comfortable taking some risks.
- Employees are coachable.
- Your organization is comfortable discussing the challenges that it's facing.

Let's take a deeper look at each of those contexts...

There Are Lots of Younger Employees
Idealists are often terrific leaders when it comes to guiding younger employees, including the Millennial generation. Idealists not only possess the learning orientation that aligns with Millennials' desires, but they tend to be less negative and judgmental regarding young workers.

Allegations of narcissism are one of the most frequent charges leveled against Millennial employees. A recent *Time* magazine cover story called Millennials the "Me Me Me Generation,"[7] and I've heard dozens of media commenters refer to Millennials as deluded and entitled. As you might imagine, those attitudes would make it incredibly hard to lead any employee. But calling any group of people narcissists, deluded, or entitled, is emotionally charged and attacking behavior, that only fuels more discord among the generations. Besides which, the accusation just isn't true; the data simply doesn't support it.

In Meg Whitman's Stanford talk, from which I quoted earlier, she also spoke about how critical her younger employees were to her success in transforming Hewlett Packard:

> We had to win hearts and minds of people [at HP] and get them back on the boat and believing again in the future of HP. So that was job number one. ... You know the challenge when you come into these companies is you can usually get your senior executives [on board]; you either replace them or they get on board. [Meanwhile] the early career folks or younger career, they're all over it they're like "OK this is what we want to do." It's what we call the frozen middle that you have to go figure out how you get them on board with the agenda that you're trying to achieve.[8]

As Meg notes, the younger, early career employees provide much of the energy for change initiatives. Also note that she doesn't call Millennials "deluded narcissists" or any other negative name. Like most Idealists, she embraces their energy, enthusiasm and desire for change and growth.

It's been my observation that when non-Idealist leaders feel irritation toward Millennials, it's often due to the lack of self-awareness they perceive from the younger employees. These leaders are okay with Millennials lacking skills, for example, but they can become apoplectic when they're convinced that these younger workers believe that, instead of lacking skills, their skills are actually good or even great. Here's the catch: Narcissists maintain the perception that they are competent, and usually they'll tell you that they're highly competent, which means, if younger workers are in fact guilty of narcissism, as so often charged, then we'd expect to see some high scores when we ask them about their skills abilities.

To see whether this is case, my team and I surveyed more than 3,000 employees from virtually every industry. Among the questions was one that asked survey participants to rate how their writing and communication skills stacked up against their peers. Our first discovery was that only 28% of employees aged 18 through 30, the Millennials, think that their communication skills are better than that of their peers. By contrast, 42% of people aged 41 through 50 think their communication skills are better. If Millennials were as narcissistic as some would have us think, then wouldn't most of them believe that their communication skills are better than their peers'? I look at this data and not only do I fail to see narcissism, I am somewhat inclined to think that Millennials may actually have a low self-esteem problem, or they truly have poor communication skills and they know it.

What about their writing skills? Here, Millennials are less critical of themselves, but not by much. Only 35% of people 18 through

30 think their writing skills are better than that of their peers, while 49% of people over 60 think their writing skills are better.

This data is not saying that Millennials are, or are not, great writers or communicators. Rather, what this data indicates is that younger workers do not think that they are great writers or communicators. According to this data, Millennials are not generally walking around narcissistically boasting of their skills, especially when compared to the other generations. Maybe your company does employ Millennials who are delusional narcissists, i.e., they think they're terrific, but their skills are actually sorely lacking. But those few bad apples shouldn't characterize an entire generation, Millennial or otherwise.

Rather than disparaging an entire generation, we should acknowledge that, as has most always been the case, younger people may enter the workforce in need of growth and development. And this is where the Idealist leadership style really shines. Idealists are high-energy achievers who believe in the positive potential of everyone around them. Idealists want to learn and grow, and they want everyone else on the team to do the same. Who better to lead younger workers than Idealists? It is all reflected in the quote that I shared earlier from David Novak at Yum!, when he stated, "People are starved for direct feedback. People want to hear how they can do better. Too many leaders don't provide that feedback. So if you take an active interest in someone, you take an active interest in sharing with them your perspective on what they can do to improve."

I recently spoke with Jeffrey Jensen Arnett, who leads the Clark University Poll of Emerging Adults: Work, Education and Identity, which surveyed a thousand 21- to 29-year-olds. Jeffrey shared with me the following study results that closely align with the data my team collected when we asked people to rate how their writing and communication skills stacked up against their peers. First, 43% of millennials, or "emerging adults," as Jeffrey calls them, feel that their education so far has them very well prepared for writing clearly and persuasively. And 42% feel very well prepared to read and understand complex information. You could look at this and think, "Well, 42%, 43% are not too bad. In fact, it's better than I thought." Or, you may think, "Holy cow, I either better start interviewing candidates more wisely or else up my employee training."

Along these same lines, Jeffrey's study found 56% of Emerging Adults say that today's job market does not value a liberal arts educational background. Given that writing and communication are essential components of liberal arts training, I find it worrisome that younger employees don't place more value on those skills, especially when I hear companies complain every day that "younger employees can't write."

A few more interesting data points from Jeffrey's study include...

- More than 3 in 5 Emerging Adults are currently unhappy with either their work-life balance, salary, or both.
- 70% of Emerging Adults have not made as much progress in their careers as they would have hoped.
- Although their ideal job would pay a lot of money, when push comes to shove, 59% of Emerging Adults would choose a job they love, even at a lower pay grade.

The boundaries that define a generation are getting narrower as the speed of the world increases. The younger employees that threaten to shake up the status quo in today's organizations are just the forerunners of many generations to come. Millennials may not operate in the work environment the same way as preceding generations, but it doesn't mean that they do not want to work. In fact, the data clearly shows that many of them want to work hard to get better at what they do.

According to a recent survey from Progressive Insurance and Wakefield Research, 81% of Millennials interested in a new job in IT would accept a less attractive compensation package to do work they are more passionate about. 82% are even willing to relocate for a job in which they are interested, and on average, they'd be willing to move more than 600 miles. It's easy to imagine these younger workers responding positively to an Idealist leadership style; remember Meg Whitman relating, "I was all about going to the best companies to get the best training to prepare for what I believed would be a long career."

There are many myths about younger workers; they're narcissistic, unwilling to learn, unwilling to relocate, etc. But as the data from my team, Clark University and Progressive show, we need to rethink these myths. Maybe Millennials don't have every ounce of preparation we'd like them to have, but if we make continual, concerted and honest efforts to teach them, mobilizing the Idealist leadership style, then we'll earn and keep their trust. And, given the increasing number of younger generation employees in our workplaces, that's a huge competitive advantage.

Employees Are Comfortable Taking Some Risks

Embracing learning and growth opportunities requires being comfortable with taking some risks. It's not the same level of risk as, say, gambling your life savings in Las Vegas, but learning and growth do require a willingness to leave your comfort zone and stretch into some new areas. For an Idealist leader to be maximally successful, it's good to have followers who are comfortable doing just that.

It seems ideal, but there's a problem. In one of my studies, I asked people how they feel about taking risks, and I offered them three possible choices by which to respond:

- I like taking risks.
- I would take a risk if it seemed prudent.
- I avoid risks.

Over all, about 28% of respondents said that they like taking risks. Clearly, not everyone is a risk taker, and that's fine. But for those who are ambitious and aspire to advance much further in their careers, taking risks is likely to be at least somewhat necessary. This became evident when I dissected the data by position. For instance, 40% of top executives like taking risks, but for frontline employees, that number is only 24%. So, in the average company, the CEO is 66% more likely to enjoy taking risks than the employees.

I'll be the first to admit that correlation doesn't always equal causation, but in this case, the differences are so stark that it's evident that being a top executive and taking risks are at least moderately linked. For the Idealist leader, this means they will find more willing followers among those who like taking some risks. These are the people who will more readily embrace learning and growth opportunities. If there is a large block of employees sufficiently ambitious that they are willing to take some risks, leave their comfort zone, and embrace personal growth, then the Idealist leadership style is likely to resonate strongly.

Employees Are Coachable
The Idealist's learning orientation typically enjoys the warmest reception amongst those who are coachable. Coachability is the ability to accept and implement feedback from bosses, colleagues, customers and others. But it goes deeper than that; coachability means that there is always something more to work on and improve. It's the drive to never be satisfied with the status quo and the belief that there are always opportunities for improvement. Given this definition, it's fairly obvious why coachable people would respond positively as followers of the Idealist.

The leaders I've discussed thus far, including Meg Whitman, Warren Buffett and Bill Gates, all display high degrees of coachability. You can also find wonderful examples of coachability

outside of the business world, for example, Tom Brady. I grew up in Buffalo, New York, so when it comes to the NFL, I'm a life-long Buffalo Bills fan. I currently live in Atlanta, Georgia, so I'm also an adopted Atlanta Falcons fan. Both loyalties mean that there aren't many who have more reason to dislike New England Patriots quarterback Tom Brady than me. And yet, I must admit that I feel immense respect for his coachability.

Yes, he's a great quarterback, with vision, smarts and the ability to throw a perfect spiral. But that's not actually what makes him so remarkable; it's his coachability. When I conducted the hiring study that inspired my book, *Hiring for Attitude: A Revolutionary Approach to Recruiting Star Performers with Both Tremendous Skills and Superb Attitude,* my team and I tracked 5,247 hiring managers from 312 public, private, business and healthcare organizations. Collectively, these managers hired more than 20,000 employees during the study period. We found that 46% of newly-hired employees will fail (i.e., be fired, receive poor performance reviews or are written up) within 18 months of hire, while only 19% will achieve unequivocal success. Contrary to popular belief, sub-par technical skills are not the primary reason why new hires fail. Poor interpersonal skills dominate the list, flaws which many of their managers admit were overlooked during the job interview process.

The study found that 26% of new hires fail because they can't accept or anticipate feedback (i.e., low coachability), 23% because they're unable to understand and manage emotions, 17% because they lack the necessary motivation to excel, 15% because they have the wrong temperament for the job, and only 11% because they lack the necessary technical skills.[9]

It's the coachability piece that makes Tom Brady so special. For example, when Brady famously said "You wanna know which ring is my favorite? The next one," he was stating that he will never be content with just having come this far. In fact, he has said exactly that: "I didn't come this far to only come this far, so we've still got further to go."[10] There have been other quarterbacks in the NFL who can throw a perfect pass, but it's arguable that there haven't been any who combined Tom Brady's physical talents with drive at quite the same intensity. So, the big question for us mere mortals is, "Do we have similar drive to keep getting better?" Or, to put it another way, "Are we as coachable as Tom Brady?" This is important, because the more coachable we are, then the more likely we are to embrace the coaching that the Idealist provides.

Here's a simple way to test coachability: Think about your boss at your last job and ask yourself, "Is there anything that I could have done, or done differently, to make our working relationship even better?" For many people, the answer is a simple, "Nah, we had a pretty good relationship, so I don't think there's much more I could have done." Others will say, "Well, my boss was the one with all the problems, so I really couldn't have done much to fix them." Unfortunately, both of those answers are evidence of a lack of coachability. Let's say that the previous boss really was the one with all the problems. Even with that, is there really nothing that could have been done better? Maybe learning some new "managing up" skills to create a better relationship with the boss? Or speaking differently to the boss during meetings? Or better anticipating the boss' moods, in order to nip some of the problems in the bud?

There is nearly always something that we can do better in workplace situations. The difference between most people and someone like Tom Brady is that Brady is a lot more likely to scour those situations to identify exactly what he could have done better, and then start working to make improvements. There's a dangerous natural tendency to blame others for what happens to us. There are bosses who really are jerks; I'm not disputing that. But I am cautioning that a knee-jerk reaction to blame everything on the boss obscures our own personal growth opportunities.

Even situations in which the previous boss was great still present a challenge, because there are many people who are quite content to say, "Yeah, it was all good, there's nothing I would have changed." It's this line of thinking that drives a complacency that all but guarantees that someone never gets any better. Perhaps the relationship really was fantastic, but as before, is there nothing that could have been done to make it even better? For example, I have a great marriage, but really, is there nothing I could do to make it even better? Maybe I could be more thoughtful, better anticipate when the garbage needs to go out, or keep my area of the kitchen counter a little neater. Once again, there is always something we can do better.

Idealist leaders really shine when their followers are coachable. It's easy to recognize the Idealist style in the example where Sheryl Sandberg told the women from the Treasury Department to sit at the table. But it's every bit as important to remember that, "At first, [the women] seemed surprised, then they agreed." Think about how much less compelling this story would have been, had the women from the Treasury Department told her to "buzz off." Fortunately for Sheryl, and all of us, these women were, like Tom Brady, highly coachable.

Your Organization Is Comfortable Discussing the Challenges That It's Facing

It is easier to succeed as an Idealist leader inside an organization that practices truthfulness and candor with its employees. David Novak said as much when he noted that, "People are starved for direct feedback," and, "Too many leaders don't provide that feedback."[11] Of course, an Idealist leader can be successful in an organizational culture that's more comfortable with obfuscation than transparency; it's just that the job is a bit harder without transparency.

One of my studies found that only 15% of employees believe that their organization "Always" openly shares the challenges facing it, while 21% state that their organization "Never" does.

Even if we combine those who say that their organization "Always" (15%) or "Frequently" (20%) openly shares the challenges, nearly two-thirds (65%) of employees still feel that their organization does not openly communicate.

When an organization is open about its challenges, it reinforces the idea that direct feedback is encouraged. Obviously, direct feedback is an essential ingredient in furthering the Idealist's aim of helping people to grow and develop. And, not surprisingly, when a company openly shares its challenges, employees are significantly more engaged. When we asked employees whether or not they would recommend their company as a great organization to work for, we discovered that 63% of employees who believe that their organization "Always" openly shares the challenges facing it, will strongly recommend it as a great organization to work for. By contrast, only 6% of employees who think their organization "Never" openly shares the challenges facing it will strongly recommend it as a great place to work. In essence, if an employee believes that their company openly communicates, then they're about 10 times more likely to endorse it as a great employer.

WARNING SIGNS THAT THE IDEALIST STYLE ISN'T WORKING

At first blush, it might seem like there is very little downside to adopting an Idealist leadership style; after all, who can really complain about being pushed to learn and grow? While it's true that the there is a lower risk of pushing the Idealist style too far than with the other three leadership styles, there are actually cases where it happens. As a starting point, here are two signs that your Idealist style may not be working...

Warning Sign #1: Middle Performers Struggle or Quit

Middle performers are those employees who do good solid work, but who have not made the leap to doing truly great work. Idealists often look at middle performers with a gleam in their eyes as they imagine all the wonderful potential they can unleash. Sometimes it works brilliantly, but there are other occasions in which a middle performer simply doesn't want, or is unable, to make the leap to high performer. In these situations, pushing the middle performer to learn and grow, no matter how good the intentions, can backfire.

My research shows that only a small percentage of middle performers are maxed out, already operating at peak efficiency and with no hope of improvement. For example, I'm well aware of my own running abilities, so I know that no matter how much I train, I will never run a four-minute mile. If that's what it takes to be a high performer at running, then I will never be a high performer. And if I'm maxed out, then pushing me to grow and develop to reach the four-minute mile is likely to frustrate both me and the Idealist coaching me.

There are also middle performers who have the potential to grow and develop, but they lack the requisite desire. Some middle performers may look at your high performers and think, "Being a high performer is a miserable existence. High performers work all weekend, are constantly pulling all-nighters and they volunteer for every shift known to mankind. It's an awful job and I'm not willing to pay that price." There are also middle performers who will exert high-performer levels of energy on work that interests and benefits them, but not on work that isn't particularly fulfilling or that doesn't excite and inspire them.

The Idealist leader can achieve remarkable results with eager-to-learn, ambitious, coachable employees. But when someone is truly maxed out, or has no desire to grow, then pushing them to learn can backfire. Some people truly want to show up to work, do a decent (but not great) job, go home and stop thinking about work. Others want to grow, but they just aren't succeeding. If an Idealist pushes either of those groups of middle performers too hard, those employees may disengage or even quit.

To assess your risk of being too intense with your middle performers, especially with middle performers who you believe have untapped potential, try using this script: "I want to tell you that your performance has been very solid, successfully meeting all expectations. But I also would like you to know that I believe that you have untapped potential. I've gotten a sense of how talented you are, and I'd like to talk about finding ways to tap that potential. Is this a conversation you feel OK having?" If your middle performers say "No," or "I'm not comfortable having that conversation," it tells you that your Idealist style might be pushing them a bit too far.

Warning Sign #2: Goals Are Causing Too Much Anxiety

When an employee is challenged to grow and develop by their Idealist boss, that employee is bound to feel a little trepidation. That's not a bad thing. Think about the most significant and meaningful accomplishments in your life, whether professional or personal. Maybe it's, "When I started a new business," or "The day I ran a marathon," or "Standing in the starting gate at the Olympics," or "That breakthrough product I invented," or "When I nursed my sick child back to health," or "When I got my college degree." Identify the victories that have been the most important to you.

Based on your response, consider the following: Were those accomplishments easy or difficult to achieve? Did I exert a little or a lot of effort? Did I already know everything that I needed to know when I started out, or did I have to learn new skills to succeed? Was I completely worry free, or did I have a few doubts or even some nervousness along the way? Most people find that every noteworthy accomplishment they've ever achieved was difficult. It was hard to do, demanded a lot of effort, they had to learn new subject matter or skills, and they had moments of worry.

Difficult goals work because they force us to pay attention; we can't simply sleepwalk through them. Maybe they arouse our attention because they're a little scary, really exciting, or they're a major departure from our normal daily routine. Whatever the reason, difficult goals get our brains worked up, and that's how to reach a level of great performance.

There is, however, such a thing as too much anxiety, and it often occurs if you have absolutely no idea what you're doing. For example, imagine that you have never played piano. (Obviously, if you really have never played piano, no imagination is necessary.) Now, let's say I give you a goal of playing an intermediate piece, for instance, Beethoven's *"Für Elise."* If you don't know the work, look it up and you'll immediately recognize this familiar classical melody. So, you've been given the goal of playing *"Für Elise"* and you've got zero experience playing the piano. You will probably start by staring at the music for a while, trying to figure out the notes. Maybe you'll try humming the melody. Then, bit by bit, you might start to cobble together a few phrases, trying to match the notes of the melody with the keys on the piano. You might even succeed in banging out a few notes that sound a little like *"Für Elise,"* but your technique will not be good, you won't use the right fingerings, and it will be sloppy. Even if you make your way through a few lines of music, you will greatly undercut your long-term ability to play piano. If I give you a goal to play *"Für Elise"* and you don't know how to play piano, like any normal person given a similar challenge, you will probably take every shortcut available to play that piece, even if it means using inferior technique and developing some bad habits.

Similarly, if you don't golf and I give you a goal of breaking 100, you might go out and buy every wonder club, try every swing gimmick, get the biggest driver, buy all the magazines, etc. And not only will you probably not break 100, but you won't learn the fundamentals, such as a slow backswing, keeping your head down, proper extension, and so on. The first golf teacher I had when I was a kid made it very clear to me: No fancy drivers until you've mastered a 5 iron. And yet, every 100+ golfer on the planet has the coolest, biggest driver available, with which they hit good drives maybe 10% of the time, all the while violating the fundamental mechanics of a golf swing and destroying their hopes for future success.

In both of these examples, the inevitable failures are not the result of setting difficult goals; they're the result of setting performance goals. Performance goals focus on achieving a desired end result, such as a golf score under 100 or playing *"Für Elise."* In contrast, a learning goal is less fixated on breaking 100 or playing *"Für Elise,* and more dedicated to learning the necessary fundamentals so that you'll eventually break 100 or play the Beethoven. When you are truly starting at ground zero, and when you have absolutely no idea how to accomplish what you are trying to do, a performance goal can backfire. If you know, for example, that a key opens doors and a driver is the guy picking you up at the airport, but you have no understanding of what these terms mean with respect to playing the piano or golf, then you probably should start with a learning goal. However, if you can read music, and you know the difference between a driver and a 3-wood, then you may be ready for performance goals.

In situations in which someone is truly starting at the beginning, then your best bet, as their Idealist leader, is to make their goals difficult, but in a learning environment. If someone doesn't know how to golf, for example, don't assign the goal of breaking 100. That's a performance goal and it probably will not work for people who truly have no strategies for accomplishing that goal. Instead, set a learning goal, maybe that starts with learning the basics of grip, posture and stance, before progressing to work on the back swing while keeping the head down and the body centered, etc. And, as part of that learning goal, have the person practice each component 100 times while analyzing and correcting each practice.

SHOULD YOU EVER TRY TO BECOME MORE OF AN IDEALIST?

Even if the Idealist isn't your default leadership style, there are times when you might consider employing some of the Idealist characteristics described heretofore.

Perhaps you're leading a team of young, smart employees and you're worried about keeping them energized and engaged. Maybe you need more innovation to stay ahead of your competitors. Or, it may be that you need a group of employees to help drive a major change effort. These are just a few of the many situations in which you might decide to employ a bit more of the Idealist leadership style. Here are three techniques to get you started:

Idealist Technique #1: Have Learning Conversations

There is a strong, positive relationship between how much people learn on the job and how much they love their job. For example, employees who score high on the survey question, "I will have to learn new skills to achieve my assigned goals for this year," have higher scores on questions such as:

- I consider myself a high performer.
- The work I do makes a difference in people's lives.
- I recommend this company to others as a great place for people to work.
- I recommend my boss to others as a great person to work for.

Unfortunately, we know from the research in my book, *HARD Goals*, that only 42% of workers say they are "Always" or "Frequently" learning on the job, while another 39% say they are "Never" or "Rarely" learning. We also know that nearly 50% of people will not have to learn new skills before they'll be able to accomplish their goals this year.[12]

119

Borrowing the technique of learning conversations favored by the Idealist leader allows you to correct this. Simply hold monthly conversations where you ask employees the following four questions that encourage and ensure new learning. Make sure that you write everything down as you go, as a way of tracking employee progress.

Question #1: "What things would you like to get better at this next month?"
This goal-focused question lets employees know that you want them to grow and that there are cool things on the horizon that they can learn. It also establishes the expectation that learning, growth and development are all job requirements. The most productive people are goal driven, but when we asked survey respondents, "My goals for this year will help me maximize my full potential," only 13% strongly agreed. Setting challenging goals forces people to learn new things. Goal-setting shouldn't be a perfunctory, once a year activity conducted during an annual performance review. Goal-setting should be an ongoing activity. Set a one- or two-month goal and ask employees, "What will you have to learn to achieve this goal?" If there is no new learning, then increase the difficulty of the goal. Regularly asking this question will ensure that your people are learning all the time.

Question #2: "What things are you better at now than you were last month?"
Setting challenging goals is a great way to enforce learning, but if people don't realize what they've learned, then the experience falls flat. Formal training programs are a great means of new learning, but so are the subtler, on-the-job learning experiences that often get missed. Asking, "What things are you better at now than you were last month?" nudges employees to recall all of the

learning they have experienced, for example, new negotiating skills, more efficient time management.

Questions #3 and #4: "Could you tell me about a time in the past month when you felt excited?" and "Could you tell me about a time in the past month when you felt demotivated?"

There is no one-size-fits-all method for keeping your people brimming with the level of new learning and passion that inspires best efforts. Asking individual employees about their demotivating "Shoves" and motivating "Tugs" provides clues about employee passions and what people should be learning.

Questions 3 and 4 are designed to ask about specific moments in the past month. This is different from asking the abstract question, "What motivates you and what demotivates you?" Abstract questions generally prompt equally abstract responses, for example, "I love being fulfilled" or "I don't like being micromanaged." When you ask about a specific time in the past thirty days, you will hear a specific response, for example: "Last month when I was working on the ACME project, I had to take over the team for a week when Pat was out sick. It was an incredible experience that really pushed me hard, but the team responded to my leadership, and the client personally thanked me for my work. I honestly can't remember ever feeling that pumped up about work before." This is the type of specific response that tells you a lot about what this person loves doing and wants to do more of. It's easy to build learning goals when you've got this level of information.

Taking the time to have the simple, four-part learning conversation, outlined above, with employees every month goes far in making sure that your people are stretching and growing professionally. When your people are learning, you can be assured that you are tapping into that Idealist leadership style.

Idealist Technique #2: Inspire Innovation

Did you know that it was Google engineers and not the auto industry that started the race to produce a self-driving car? While the concept of an autonomous car dates back to at least the 1920s, it was Google engineers who matched a well-documented human pain: driver error causes millions of traffic deaths, with the building blocks of a solution: Google Maps, Google Earth and Street View. Granted, the technology still has a way to go before you and I can safely hit the road hands-off, but the point I'm driving here is about innovation. How can today's leaders motivate employees to embrace the kind of thinking that gives great organizations like Google the first-mover advantage?

An Idealist leader gives employees the permission to learn; it's the first step in inspiring innovation. Sadly, I still encounter too many organizations that claim they desire and support innovation, but whose leaders are killing creative thinking. For example, distributing a memo or initiating a command that states, "Here's what's happening and here's what I want you to do about it," prevents people from tapping into their full potential, because it's not asking employees to truly think independently; it's not empowering. More than a third of leaders operate in this manner.

As a leader, it's your job to motivate people to go places they wouldn't otherwise go—but when you tell employees where to go, and how to get there, it squashes the desire to come up with their own great ideas. I am not suggesting that you let everyone roam free, but innovative thinking must be more than a warm and fuzzy idea. Your people should feel a certain level of pressure when it comes to innovative thinking.

This quote from a Google employee blogging about Google's 20% Time, where employees take time out of their core jobs to be creative and experimental on work of their own choosing, sums it up nicely: "This [20% Time] isn't a matter of doing something in your spare time, but of more actively making time for it. Heck,

I don't have a good 20% project yet and I need one. If I don't come up with something I'm sure it could negatively impact my review."[13] Google's 20% Time isn't a casual and fun option to innovate. For those employees to whom it is assigned, it's an expected, high-challenge requirement.

There are many effective, non-confrontational methods of applying pressure on your people to innovate. Article reading contests, for example, are a more relaxed way to encourage employees to procure their own information about the marketplace, your competitors, the quality of the organization's products and your customers. Start by determining an issue for which you would like to raise employee awareness, for example competitor pricing, customer service or teamwork. Then ask employees to bring in a relevant article on the topic and to be prepared to talk about their selected article. Announce that whoever brings in the best article wins a prize. Don't get discouraged if only a few people participate the initial time. Once word spreads that all it takes to get dinner out or a movie on the company, is to bring in an article and be able to talk about it, participation will pick up. Companies that participate in article reading contests find that the exercise prompts employees, on their own, to engage in productive debates about the big issues facing the organization and to join forces to find solutions.

Experience-sharing across management levels is another way to foster innovation. Once a month, gather colleagues from multiple levels of the organization, and ask someone to present an issue, for example, cutting costs. Then, open a group discussion. Someone might present the issue, "I tried cutting costs by hiring outside contractors and here are the good and bad lessons I learned..." Once the issue is introduced, then others can share their stories and experiences around this topic. Experience sharing, unlike unsolicited advice, makes people more open to actually hearing and processing information. It triggers a thought process—"That's a great idea, I'm going to try that," or "That really went wrong. I don't want to do it like that. I'm going to try something different."

Asking employees to keep a Best Practice Journal is yet another constructive way to inspire employees to learn by observing what's happening around them. Ask them to document examples of great performance as they see it happening out in the world, and make time for sharing these observations at regular staff meetings. For example, someone might record in their journal, "I observed a manager reviewing the new work schedule with two cashiers while I was out shopping. One cashier unhappily said, 'Wait, so Tory gets to work days and I get stuck with evening hours.' The manager very calmly replied, 'We are here to talk about your schedule, not Tory's.' I watched the cashier's face grimace for a second and then she just relaxed and focused on the schedule and the manager led her through it, with no argument. It was remarkable to see how simple, neat, non-aggressive and effective this approach was, and I plan to do the same thing the next time I'm in a similar situation." Documenting and sharing best practices inspires new ways of observing and new avenues of thinking.

The lesson here for aspiring Idealists is that the more you empower your people to learn, the more innovative, fulfilled and smarter they'll become—and that translates to greater organizational success.

Idealist Technique #3: Get Employees More Comfortable with Taking Risks

We know that for an employee to be fully inspired by the Idealist leadership style and great learning and growth opportunities, they must be willing to take some risks and leave their comfort zone. The good news is that you can gently nudge people to embrace a little more risk by having them complete the following three-step exercise:

Risk-Taking Step 1: Think about this past year, recalling situations in which you opted to take a safer course of action. Maybe it was a meeting at which you kept quiet about your big idea. Or the tough feedback that you didn't give a colleague. Or when you didn't volunteer to present at the executive team meeting. Regardless of the specifics, most people can look back over twelve months and find at least a few times when they opted for a less risky option.

Risk-Taking Step 2: Ask yourself why you didn't take the riskier path. What stops people from taking a risk often seems at first to be a fear of failure. For example, I could say that I didn't pitch my big idea at the meeting because I was afraid it would be rejected. But that fear of rejection is really masking a deeper fear; namely that, "I'll die from embarrassment," or "I'm not as smart/talented/ skilled as I think I am," or "This is my only shot at this and if I screw up I'll never get another chance."

Some fear is very healthy. From an evolutionary perspective, fear of saber-toothed tigers, for instance, triggered a flight response that helped to prevent early humans from being eaten alive. But if you take a risk to pitch your idea in a meeting and it is rejected, the embarrassment you feel probably won't kill you. Most of the repercussions we face if we fail, when taking a risk, won't really kill us; they're interpretations, assumptions, emotionally charged extrapolations, catastrophizing, or irrational beliefs. They are not typically life-and-death consequences.

Risk-Taking Step 3: Commit to taking a risk next month or next year that you would have avoided this month or this year. By "commit," you should write down, on a piece of paper, a pledge such as, "I'm going to pitch my new product idea at the team meeting on January 15th." Once you've written it down, put this note on your desk where you can't help but see it every day and then get to work preparing your pitch.

Being an Idealist leader doesn't require employees to take monumental risks every day; no cliff diving is required. But for employees to embrace the Idealist's learning and growth philosophy, they do need to venture outside of their comfort zone, even if just a little. By having your employees complete this exercise, you're asking them to find small opportunities to stretch and take a risk; nothing outlandish, just baby steps. But step-by-step, as employees become more comfortable, and their risk-taking leads to success, they will become more responsive to the Idealist leadership style.

WHAT TYPES OF EMPLOYEES DO AND DON'T WORK WELL WITH THE IDEALIST

My research has revealed several characteristics that positively correlate with idealizing the Idealist leadership style. I discovered these characteristics by assessing and analyzing the personality characteristics of employees and then measuring how they respond to the Idealist leadership style. Here's what I found:

People who set career or business goals that others describe as "difficult" or "audacious," and who would rather take on a challenging and difficult project, as opposed to one that they are confident they can complete, tend to respond better to the Idealist. Given how much the Idealist wants people to learn, grow and develop, this isn't terribly surprising.

We also discovered that those who idealize the Idealist leadership style are more likely to enjoy being part of a group or team and working with others. While the Idealist is pushing people to grow and develop, it is done out of a sense of caring for that person. And the Idealist doesn't help just one person; they're often focused on developing as many as they can. It only makes sense that the Idealist's followers would share that caring and comradery.

Along those same lines, the Idealist's followers tend to be more tolerant and forgiving. Given that these people will be learning, trying new things and even making mistakes, being tolerant and forgiving is a good attribute to have. And, as we might expect, the Idealist's followers are more likely to be accepting of people with different views and opinions.

CONCLUSION

I hope that this book has impacted the way you think about leadership styles in at least four ways.

First, at the most basic level, I wrote this book to teach readers about the range of available leadership styles. While the phrase, "leadership styles" is ubiquitous, especially throughout the management training industry, this book presents the first truly detailed investigation of each of the leadership styles, including how they work in real-life scenarios.

In decades past, there have been descriptions of autocratic, democratic or laissez-faire leadership styles, just to name a few. But those categorizations were so obviously bad or good in their one-size-fits all approach, that every successful leader has virtually no choice but to identify with the same category. My first goal in writing this book was to share a framework whereby we can understand, in detail, various approaches to leadership with more subtlety and nuance. Tim Cook from Apple, Sheryl Sandberg from Facebook, and Jeff Bezos from Amazon are all successful leaders, but their approaches are sufficiently different that they fall into distinct leadership style categories.

Pragmatists are driven, competitive, and they value hitting their goals above all else, while Diplomats are kind, social, and build deep personal bonds with their employees. Idealists want to learn and grow, and they desire that everyone else on the team to do the same, while Stewards value rules, process and cooperation. One style is not, a priori, universally better than another; each style has its own strengths, weaknesses and situational advantages. If readers understand those differences, then my primary goal has been achieved.

A second goal of this book was to demonstrate that one universal leadership style does not exist. Contrary to what some would have you believe, there is no one right way or one perfect approach to be a successful leader. Not every leader is going to handwrite 8,000 birthday cards a year like Sheldon Yellen. Or read five to six hours a day like Warren Buffett. Or exhort employees to "throw a pie in the face of all the naysayers on Wall Street" like Elon Musk. I am hoping that what you have learned from this book, with its variety of examples and techniques, is that there are many good ways to lead.

Third, this book should help leaders and would-be leaders understand the strengths and weaknesses of their own styles. Some leadership styles are more effective for retaining and engaging employees, while other styles are more effective when a team is highly creative but not achieving tangible results. Some approaches work better when employees are comfortable taking some risks, while others are more suited to alleviating employee burnout. Not only is it critical to know which styles work best in a given situation, it is important to understand which style aligns with how you are naturally inclined to lead. Knowing that you're best at leading ambitious and competitive go-getters, for example, might indicate that you need to exercise a great deal of self-awareness if you're suddenly tasked with leading a group of emotionally fragile, burnt-out employees.

Finally, as a result of this book, I would like leaders to recognize how they can adapt to situations that arise by using techniques from across the four styles. I'm regularly asked whether or not it's possible for a leader to change their leadership style. The answer is, "It depends," because the ability to change styles, or incorporate components of other styles, has much to do with the leader's level of self-awareness. It may not be necessary to radically change an entire leadership style. For example, it's often not a great use of a Pragmatist's time to try to completely remake themselves into a Diplomat. But it doesn't mean that the Pragmatists can't employ some of the Diplomat's tactics, such as conducting Shoves and Tugs conversations. In describing some of the techniques of each of the four leadership styles, I hope that leaders see how they can tweak their current leadership style to meet specific situations.

This book should mark the starting point of your exploration of leadership styles, not the end point. I have been studying the topic of leadership styles for years and still continue to learn something new every day. To that end, I invite you continue with me on this intellectual journey; let's keep learning and growing together! Keep in touch and follow my latest work on leadership styles at www.leadershipiq.com/leadershipstyles.

ABOUT THE AUTHOR

Mark Murphy is a *New York Times* bestselling author, contributor to *Forbes* and *CNBC*, and founder of Leadership IQ, a research and training firm.

Mark is ranked as one of the Top 30 leadership gurus in the world, and some of his most well-known research studies include "Are SMART Goals Dumb?," "Why CEOs Get Fired," "Why New Hires Fail," "High Performers Can Be Less Engaged," and "Don't Expect Layoff Survivors to Be Grateful."

Mark leads one of the world's largest databases of original leadership research, and his work has appeared in the *Wall Street Journal*, the *New York Times, Fortune, Forbes, Bloomberg Businessweek*, and *U.S. News & World Report*. Mark has also appeared on CNN, NPR, CBS *Sunday Morning*, ABC's *20/20*, and the Fox Business Network.

Mark has lectured at the United Nations, Harvard Business School, the Clinton Foundation, Microsoft, Merck, MasterCard, Charles Schwab, Aflac, and hundreds more.

Mark's most recent books include *Leadership Styles: How to Discover and Leverage Yours* and *Truth At Work: The Science of Delivering Tough Messages*. He is the author of the *New York Times* bestseller *Hundred Percenters: Challenge Your People to Give It Their All and They'll Give You Even More.* Before that, his book *Hiring for Attitude* was featured in *Fast Company* and the *Wall Street Journal* and was chosen as a top business book by CNBC.

Some of his other books include *HARD Goals: The Science of Getting from Where You Are to Where You Want to Be* and *The Deadly Sins of Employee Retention.*

FOR MORE INFORMATION

For free downloadable resources including quizzes and discussion guides, please visit www.leadershipiq.com

NOTES

INTRODUCTION
1 Greenstein, Fred I. "The Virtuosic Leadership of Franklin D. Roosevelt." *The Presidential Difference: Leadership Style from FDR to Barack Obama*, 18. New Jersey: Princeton University Press, 2012.

CHAPTER 1
1 Ayre, James. *"Tesla CEO Elon Musk's August 29 Email to Employees Calls for 3rd Quarter Rally for Profitability (Full Email Text)."* CleanTechnica, September 7, 2016. https://cleantechnica. com/2016/09/07/tesla-ceo-elon-musks-august-29-email-employ-ees-calls-3rd-quarter-rally-profitability-full-email-text/.

2 Murphy, Mark. *HARD Goals.* New York, USA: McGraw-Hill Professional Publishing, 2010.

3 Maney, Kevin. "Q&A with Jeff Bezos: Risk-Taking and Customer Value." *Seeking Alpha.* August 24, 2008. https://seekingalpha. com/article/73725-q-and-a-with-jeff-bezos-risk-taking-and-cus-tomer-value.

4 Dyer, Jeff, and Hal Gregersen. "The Secret to Unleashing Genius." *Forbes,* August 14, 2013. https://www.forbes.com /sites/innovatorsdna/2013/08/14/the-secret-to-unleashing-genius/#2de5b57a361c/.

5 Musk, Elon. "Master Plan, Part Deux." *Tesla | Premium Electric Sedans and SUVs* (blog). July 20, 2016. https://www.tesla.com/ blog/master-plan-part-deux/.

6 Ong, Josh. "Elon Musk on Fear, Failure, and His Close Calls with SpaceX, Tesla." *The Next Web* (blog). November 1, 2013. https://thenex-tweb.com/entrepreneur/2013/10/31/elon-musk-failure-fear/.

7 Sheff, David. "Playboy Interview: Steven Jobs." *Playboy Magazine,* February 1985, 49.

8 Blodget, Henry. "14 Years Ago Jeff Bezos Told You How to Take Over The World." *Business Insider,* November 16, 2011. https://www.businessinsider.com/jeff-bezos-told-you-how-to-take-over-the-world-2011-11.

9 Murphy, Mark. "If Your Employees Aren't Learning, You're Not Leading." *Forbes,* January 21, 2018. https://www.forbes.com/ sites/markmurphy/2018/01/21/if-your-employees-arent-learning-youre-not-leading/#74b403a09478.

10 Dubner, Stephen J. "'Never Follow Your Dreams: Mark Cuban Answers Your Questions." *Freakonomics* (blog). February 3, 2012. http://freakonomics.com/2012/02/03/never-follow-your-dreams-mark-cuban-answers-your-questions/.

11 Stone, Brad. "The Secrets of Bezos: How Amazon Became the Everything Store." *Bloomberg,* October 10, 2013. https://www.

bloomberg.com/news/articles/2013-10-10/jeff-bezos-and-the-age-of-amazon-excerpt-from-the-everything-store-by-brad-stone.

12 The Mayo Clinic Staff. "Know the Signs of Job Burnout." *Mayo Clinic.* Last modified September 17, 2015. https://www.mayo-clinic.org/healthy-lifestyle/adult-health/in-depth/burnout/art-20046642.

13 Bryant, Adam. "Erika Nardini On the Value of Leading '10 Percent' Players." *The New York Times,* July 14, 2017, The Corner Office. https://www.nytimes.com/2017/07/14/business/erika-nardini-barstool-sports-value-of-leading-10-percent-players.html.

14 Snyder, Bill. "Walmart CEO: Waiting for Consensus 'Can Kill You'" *Stanford Graduate School of Business,* March 23, 2015. https://www.gsb.stanford.edu/insights/walmart-ceo-waiting-consensus-can-kill-you.

15 Murphy, Mark. "If Your Employees Aren't Learning, You're Not Leading." *Forbes.* January 21, 2018. https://www.forbes.com/sites/markmurphy/2018/01/21/if-your-employees-arent-learning-youre-not-leading/#4f27c9169478.

16 MacMahon, Tim. "'The Gift and the Curse' Fueling Chris Paul's Competitive Fire." *ESPN.com* (blog). January 15, 2018. http://www.espn.com/nba/story/_/id/22098380/chris-paul-competitive-fire-gift-curse-houston-rockets-point-guard-nba.

CHAPTER 2
1 Weller, Chris. "A CEO Who Writes 8,000 Employee Birthday Cards a Year Just Got the Ultimate 'Thank You.'" *Business Insider,* January 18, 2018. http://www.businessinsider.com/ceo-writes-8000-birthday-cards-a-year-gets-ultimate-thank-you-2018-1.

2 Ibid.

3 Ibid.

4 Ward, Marguerite. "Why the CEO of a $1.5 Billion Dollar Company Doesn't Use a Smart Phone." CNBC, July 26, 2016. https://www.cnbc.com/2016/07/26/why-the-ceo-of-a-15-billion-dollar-company-doesnt-use-a-smartphone.html.

5 Butt, Rachel. "This Billionaire CEO Cares About His Employees More than Investors, and the Company's Stock Is up 457% Since 2008." *Business Insider*, August 12, 2016. http://www.businessinsider.com/nidec-corps-bllionaire-chief-executive-officer-talks-about-employees-2016-8.

6 Prajapati, Jagdish. "The Man Hotter than the Sun - Inspiring Leader Mr. Nagamori." *LinkedIn* (blog), August 12, 2016. https://www.linkedin.com/pulse/man-hotter-than-sun-inspiring-leader-jagdish-prajapati/.

7 Wang, Monica. "America's Favorite CEOs in 2016, and Why Their Employees Love Them." *Forbes*, June 10, 2016. https://www.forbes.com/sites/monicawang/2016/06/10/americas-favorite-ceos-in-2016-and-why-their-employees-love-them/#87ab8f417544.

8 Smuin, Amanda. "Tech Savvy: Dr King Owyang, Executive Director & CEO of Computime." *CEO Magazine*, October 2017. https://www.theceomagazine.com/business/dr-king-owyang.

9 Benna, Steven. "17 quotes that take you inside the mind of billionaire investor Mark Cuban." *Business Insider*, September 18, 2015. http://www.businessinsider.com/best-mark-cuban-quotes-2015-9/#on-preparation-2.

10 "How Job Seekers Are Using Glassdoor." *Glassdoor for Employers*, Last modified May 23, 2017. https://www.glassdoor.com/employers/blog/how-candidates-use-glassdoor/.

11 Weiner, Jeff. "My Thoughts on the Election." *LinkedIn* (blog), November 10, 2016. https://www.linkedin.com/pulse/my-thoughts-election-jeff-weiner/.

12 "A Letter to American Employees from Doug Parker and Robert Isom on Team Member Pay." *Newsroom - Home - American Airlines Group, Inc.*, Accessed February 12, 2018. http://news.aa.com/press-releases/press-release-details/2017/A-letter-to-American-employees-from-Doug-Parker-and-Robert-Isom-on-team-member-pay/default.aspx.

13 Associated Press. "American Airlines announces pay raises, and investors balk." *Los Angeles Times*, April 27, 2017.

14 "Employee Engagement Shocker: Low Performers May Be MORE Engaged than High Performers." *Leadership IQ* (blog), (n.d.). https://www.leadershipiq.com/blogs/leadershipiq/35354881-employee-engagement-shocker-low-performers-may-be-more-engaged-than-high-performers.

15 Morris, Keiko. "New Jersey Has a Millennials Problem." *The Wall Street Journal*, July 30, 2017.

16 Ibid.

17 Lincoln, Ross A. "Bob Iger: 'The Force Awakens' "One of The Proudest" Moments in Disney History." *Deadline Hollywood*, December 16, 2015. http://deadline.com/2015/12/bob-iger-praises-star-wars-the-force-awakens-and-disney-employees-in-company-memo-1201668421/.

18 Gilman, Hank. "The Most Underrated CEO Ever The legend-ary Sam Walton got the credit, but it was David Glass who turned Wal-Mart into the world's largest company." *FORTUNE Magazine*, April 5, 2004. http://archive.fortune.com/magazines/fortune/fortune_archive/2004/04/05/366366/index.htm.

19 Ibid.

20 "Ken Chenault, CEO of American Express at View from the Top Talk (Transcript)." *The Singju Post*, April 11, 2016. https://singjupost.com/ken-chenault-ceo-of-american-express-at-view-from-the-top-talk-transcript/.

21 Ibid.

CHAPTER 3
1 Yeh, Chris. "CS183C Session 8: Eric Schmidt." *Medium*, October 16, 2015. https://medium.com/cs183c-blitzscaling-class-collection/cs183c-session-8-eric-schmidt-56c29b247998.

2 Colt, Sam. "Here's What It's Like to Work with Tim Cook." *Business Insider*, October 25, 2014. http://www.businessinsider.com/working-with-apple-ceo-tim-cook-2014-10.

3 "What's It Like Working with Tim Cook?." *Quora*, Accessed February 12, 2018. https://www.quora.com/Whats-it-like-working-with-Tim-Cook.

4 Hackett, Robert. "Why Cisco's Board Chose Chuck Robbins to Lead as CEO." *Fortune*, May 5, 2015. http://fortune.com/2015/05/05/cisco-ceo-chuck-robbins/.

5 Safian, Robert. "How CEO Mark Parker Runs Nike to Keep Pace with Rapid Change." *Fast Company*, November 5,

2012. https://www.fastcompany.com/3002642/how-ceo-mark-parker-runs-nike-keep-pace-rapid-change.

6 Weill, Sandy. "25 People to Blame for the Financial Crisis." *Time*, (n.d.). http://content.time.com/time/specials/packages/article/0,28804,1877351_1877350_1877329,00.html.

7 Elkind, Peter. "Ex-Citigroup Chief Says Bankers Behaving 'Wildly.'" *Fortune*, October 28, 2010. http://archive.fortune.com/2010/10/27/news/companies/john_reed_citigroup.fortune/index.htm.

CHAPTER 4

1 Sandberg, Sheryl and Scovell, Nell. "Sit at the Table." In *Lean In: Women, Work, and the Will to Lead*, 27-28. New York: Alfred A. Knopf, 2013.

2 Bryant, Adam. "At Yum Brands, Rewards for Good Work." *The New York Times*, July 11, 2009. http://www.nytimes.com/2009/07/12/business/12corner.html.

3 Whitman, Meg. "HP CEO Meg Whitman on Integrity & Courage in Leadership." *YouTube*, April 10, 2015. https://www.youtube.com/watch?v=gcvX-lNu1bM&feature=youtu.be.

4 Whitman, Meg. "Distinguished Speaker Series: Meg Whitman - Chairman, President and CEO of HP." *YouTube*, May 4, 2015. https://www.youtube.com/watch?v=vkmUvP79PpE&feature=youtu.be.

5 "How Warren Buffett Keeps up with a Torrent of Information." *Farnam Street* (blog), July 1, 2016. https://www.fs.blog/2015/05/warren-buffett-information/.

6 Rosman, Katherine. "Bill Gates on Books and Blogging." *The New York Times*, January 4, 2016. https://www.nytimes.com/2016/01/04/fashion/bill-gates-gates-notes-books.html.

7 Stein, Joel. "Millennials: The Me Me Me Generation." *Time*, May 20, 2013. http://time.com/247/millennials-the-me-me-me-generation/.

8 Whitman, Meg. "HP CEO Meg Whitman on Integrity & Courage in Leadership." *YouTube*. April 10, 2015. https://www.youtube.com/watch?v=gcvX-lNu1bM&feature=youtu.be.

9 Murphy, Mark A. "Why New Hires Fail (Emotional Intelligence vs. Skills)." *Leadership IQ* (blog), (n.d.). https://www.leadershipiq.com/blogs/leadershipiq/35354241-why-new-hires-fail-emotional-intelligence-vs-skills.

10 "Tom Brady's Inspirational Playoff Quote: 'I Didn't Come This Far to Only Come This Far.'" *CBS Boston* (blog). January 6, 2016. http://boston.cbslocal.com/2016/01/06/tom-bradys-inspirational-playoff-quote-i-didnt-come-this-far-to-only-come-this-far/.

11 Bryant, Adam. "At Yum Brands, Rewards for Good Work." *The New York Times*, July 11, 2009. http://www.nytimes.com/2009/07/12/business/12corner.html.

12 Murphy, Mark A. *HARD Goals: The Secret to Getting from Where You Are to Where You Want to Be.* New York: McGraw-Hill, 2011.

13 Iyer, Bala, and Thomas H. Davenport. "Reverse Engineering Google's Innovation Machine." *Harvard Business Review*, April 2008. https://hbr.org/2008/04/reverse-engineering-googles-innovation-machine.